AIR FORCE ONE

ES OF AMERICA

28000

ROBERT F. DORR

MBI Publishing Company

First published in 2002 by MBI Publishing Company, Galtier Plaza, Suite 200, 380 Jackson Street, St. Paul, MN 55101-3885 USA

MBI Publishing Company books are also available at discounts in bulk quantity for industrial or sales-promotional use. For details write to Special Sales Manager at Motorbooks International Wholesalers & Distributors, Galtier Plaza, Suite 200, 380 Jackson Street, St. Paul, MN 55101-3885 USA.

Library of Congress Cataloging-in-Publication Data Available

ISBN 0-7603-1055-6

Edited by Sara Perfetti
Cover designed by Stephanie Michaud
Designed by Jerry Stenback

Printed in China

On the front cover: Ronald and Nancy Reagan, Berlin, Germany, June 12, 1987. *Courtesy Ronald Reagan Library*

On the fronis piece: Air Force One as viewed from beneath. *Jim Kippen*

On the title page: Topeka, Kansas, September 6, 1990. George Bush's first flight in the new Air Force One. *Jerry Geer*

On the back cover: (main) SAM 29000 waits at Barksdale Air Force Base, Louisiana. *Greg L. Davis (small right)* Truman's VC-118-DO, the *Independence*. *Norman Taylor (small left)* First Lady Mamie Eisenhower christens the *Columbine III* with the traditional smashing of a bottle, on November 24, 1954. *Courtesy of the National Archives*

On the dedication/acknowledgments page: John and Jacqueline Kennedy, San Juan, Puerto Rico, December 17, 1961. *Photo number ST-285-25-61 in the John F. Kennedy Library*

AIR FORCE ONE

D E D I C A T I O N *and* A C K N O W L E D G M E N T S

AIR FORCE ONE

Air Force One is the story of a plane that belongs to a nation, and a history of presidential travel. Any errors in this book are the fault of the author. Many individuals helped to make this book possible.

A gracious former first lady, Nancy Reagan, gave this author a few minutes to share memories of Air Force One.

I have a special gratitude to former Air Force Chief of Staff General Ronald Fogleman, former Secretary of the Air Force F. Whitten Peters, and current Secretary of the Air Force Dr. James Roche for their personal encouragement of my writing. I owe a similar debt to two successive commanders of the 89th Airlift Wing: Major General James Hawkins and Colonel Glenn Spears.

I also want to thank the following members of the 89th Airlift Wing: Steve Anderson, John Atkins, Richard Balfour, Keith Blades, Dana Carroll, Bruce Christensen, Susan Coke, Rick Corral, Gene Dickson, Howie Franklin, Dennis Fritz, Jeff Gay, Vaughn Gonzales, John Haigh, Jennifer Hider, David Huxsoll, Silkya J. Irizarry, Bobby Jones, Nathan Jones, Susan Koch, Carolyn McPartlin, Kevin McQuay, Valerie Martindale, Kris Meyle, Allison Miller, Doug Normour, Heidi Ostreich, Richard Parker, Susan Richardson, Bob Ronck, Dave Rossner, Bel Serocki, Robert Shaffer, Dave Sims, Donnell Smith, Pamela Varon, Nancy Vetere, Armando Visitacion, Nicky Williams, Coennie Woods, Ronald Zaremba, and Michael Zepf.

In addition, I would like to thank the following people for their help: Kathy Bienfang, Colin Clark, Bill Crimmins, John W. Darr, Greg L. Davis, Clint Downing, Jerry Geer, Jim Goodall, John Gourley, Sunil Gupta, Joseph G. Handelman, Alex Hrapunov, Dennis R. Jenkins, Tom Kaminski, Craig Kaston, Jim Kippen, Patrick Martin, David W. Menard, Robert C. Mikesh, David Ostrowski, Jeffrey Rhodes, Barry Roop, Charles Taylor, and Jack Valenti.

Special thanks go to Robert C. Mikesh, the leading American authority on presidential aircraft, for permission to adapt material from his article in the Summer 1963 issue of the *Journal of the American Aviation Historical Society* for use in chapter two of this book. Another special nod, too, to Kirsten Tedesco, Stephanie Mitchell, and James Stemm at the Pima Air and Space Museum in Tucson, Arizona. Some of the material on presidential helicopter travel comes from the government publication *Naval Aviation News*.

Air Force One is dedicated to Marc Reid, who is finally able to straighten up and fly right.

Robert F. Dorr
Oakton, Virginia

THE FLYING WHITE HOUSE

At Andrews Air Force Base in Maryland, outside the nation's capital, the president of the United States prepares to take a trip. The sky giant that will carry the president is a marvel of engineering. Just now, the plane is indoors—the president will climb aboard while it is still inside its hangar—but to those who can see it, the aircraft catches the eye and holds the gaze.

Many Americans would recognize it as a Boeing 747, the jumbo jet that opened up air travel to the everyday citizen. This one is a military version, known in jargon as a VC-25. But there is nothing everyday about this particular aircraft and nothing obscure about the name by which most of the world knows it. To the press, to the public, to moviegoers and air enthusiasts, even to the people who work on it, it is called Air Force One.

One Air Force officer described Air Force One as "magnificent . . . like a cruise ship." Like other Boeing 747s, the flying White House has a complex, tandem, twin-bogey main landing gear that retracts quickly on takeoff. The high angle of attack is made possible by the enormous push of the four General Electric F103-GE-180 turbofan engines, each rated at 56,750 pounds thrust. Although the aircraft is not aerodynamically capable of it, the engines are powerful enough to stand the 747 on its tail and make it climb straight up.

On Air Force bases, the president enjoys the security afforded by military personnel, but the Secret Service retains primary responsibility for protecting the chief executive. During an arrival by the presidential 747, Air Force personnel are nowhere in sight, but a Secret Service agent is standing in the pilots' three o'clock position, where he can scan the immediate area around the aircraft in all directions. *John Gourley*

The two presidential 747s are rarely seen together but appear here on the Andrews ramp. This view shows both using the internal "airstairs" unique to the Air Force VC-25A. These admit the boarder at a lower level than the portable, airfield stair units (also shown beside each plane), which are the preferred method of entry for White House occupants. *Charles Taylor*

FLYING WHITE HOUSE

Air Force One glistens, its blue and white exterior polished to a bright shine. On the inside, its engines, avionics, and instruments have been tweaked to perfection. There is probably not a 747 in the world that looks so pristine or is in such flawless running order. Air Force One is maintained by the best men and women the nation can recruit for the job. As one of them says in a quick aside, good-naturedly and with considerable pride, "You do not make a mistake when working on Air Force One."

The president of the United States is the most important customer of the Air Force's 89th Airlift Wing, the resident military unit at Andrews. The wing provides transport to members of Congress, the Cabinet, and sometimes kings and kingmakers, but the president receives very special treatment. He needs to be able to communicate with anyone in the world at any time. He needs to be able to travel to any location on short notice and to change plans on zero notice. When he heads off to some distant capital to confer with an international leader, the president needs to arrive safe, comfortable, refreshed, and ready.

PRESIDENTIAL ARRIVAL

So what is it like when the president arrives at Andrews to climb aboard his flying magic carpet? It is a sight to behold, and not solely for the magnificence of the chief executive's four-engined, 85-ton Boeing aircraft.

The chosen few among the press who cover the president are asked to arrive at Andrews an hour before his departure. En route to the fenced-in outdoor area set aside for the press, everybody stops for a search. A Secret Service agent checks each individual rigorously using a hand-held metal detector. Photographers must lay their cameras on the ground and have them sniffed by a Secret Service sentry dog. Meanwhile, the crew of Air Force One has the giant jet in readiness inside the presidential hangar.

Capable of housing two Boeing 747s indoors with plenty of space to spare, this
enormous hangar facility at Andrews was
built specifically to accommodate both Air
Force One airframes plus all support and
maintenance facilities, as well as administrative offices for the Presidential Airlift
Group. The entire area is located behind
double-row barbed wire fences and is pa-
trolled by Air Force Security Forces personnel.
Jim Kippen

The special hangars used by the two VC-25A presidential aircraft at Andrews Air Force Base (in background). Motion sensors and other detection devices surround the entire complex. In the foreground is the base fire department. *Jim Kippen*

While these preparations go on, the Secret Service may order a "quiet period" (if the president is planning to speak before departure) or a "ramp freeze" (halting all aircraft movement on the west side of the Andrews' runway 01/19), but is more likely to order both. Quiet means quiet. No other aircraft can taxi on the west side or make an afterburner takeoff during a "quiet period."

Before the president arrives or Air Force One taxis out from its hangar, a vehicle from the 89th Wing's base operations center inspects the entire flight line west of the runway for FOD (foreign object damage), meaning fallen objects of any size that might be ingested by the 11-foot open intakes of Air Force One's four General Electric F103-GE-180 turbofan engines. The flight line is carefully policed for FOD anyway, but an extra FOD inspection precedes every departure by the chief executive.

If the president is coming from the White House by motorcade, Air Force people will first observe his vehicles at the Andrews main gate just off the Washington Beltway, alias Interstate 495. An advance party will have reached the gate first, and the president will be whisked through. His motorized procession heads east on Westover Street, then

south on Arnold toward the Air Force One hangar, never slowing, never pausing.

Almost always, there are at least two identical limousines in the motorcade, one of them a decoy. Always, there are at least two gloss black Chevrolet Suburban "war wagons" carrying Secret Service agents and their weaponry. While the presidential limousine goes directly to the VIP area (if a speech is contemplated) or to the hangar (if not), two sharpshooters from the Executive Protection

SAM 28000 up against the special hangars of the Presidential Airlift Group. Normally, the aircraft is parked inside rather than out. *Jim Kippen*

13

Agency (the uniformed arm of the Secret Service) are at the ready on the ledge outside the Andrews control tower—about 1,000 feet from the hangar—with 7-mm Magnum sniper rifles with scopes inside aluminum gun cases. Additional Secret Service officers occupy other key positions surrounding the area of presidential activity.

In about ninety percent of presidential departures, the chief executive does not arrive by motorcade at all. The first sign of his appearance is the throb of the presidential helicopter, Marine One—a Sikorsky VH-3H or VH-60N. Either way, the destination is the hangar where Air Force One awaits.

Inside the hangar (tall enough to accommodate the looming, 63-foot 5-inch tail of a 747) two VC-25As are awaiting their famous passenger, one of the aircraft serving as a backup. There is always a backup. If one of the 747s is temporarily out of action for any reason, including periodic depot maintenance, some other transport from the 89th Airlift Wing serves as the backup instead. During routine operations in the United States, the 89th usually does not provide a decoy aircraft. Overseas, however, it may. On rare occasion, only a handful of people know which aircraft the president will board, up to the actual time of boarding.

PRESIDENTIAL PLANE

The VC-25A, as the Air Force calls its Boeing 747-200 (Air Force One, to most of us) is a military, VIP version of the plane that changed the world. According to a survey by aviation analysts at the Los Angeles-based Ralston Institute, as recently as 1970 only 25 percent of Americans had ever been inside an aircraft. Most Americans traveled by car, by bus, or by train. A seat on an airliner was the special province of the privileged few. At that time, most airline passengers were business people or the well-to-do. The Boeing 747 changed all that. Introduced to commercial airline service in 1970, the 747 doubled passenger capacity overnight. The wide-body, or jumbo, era had arrived. Within a few years, passenger loads on the nation's interstate

Air Force One over Middle America. George W. Bush became the third president to fly in the VC-25A, the first of which was belatedly delivered to the 89th Airlift Wing in September 1990. In this early photo, the national insignia on the rear fuselage is not quite correct. The blue bar enclosing the white field and red stripe should be thicker and darker. The minor discrepancy in color was quickly rectified. *Boeing*

It is June 5, 2001, and President George W. Bush is visiting the Florida Everglades to promote his environmental package for restoring the natural habitat there. As usual, the C-20C Gulfstream lands near the airfield being used by Air Force One, but not on it. On this occasion, the C-20C was at Patrick Air Force Base, while Air Force One landed with President George W. Bush at nearby Homestead Air Reserve Base.

Inextricably linked to Air Force One and kept strictly out of the public's eye are the Air Force's three C-20C Gulfstream IVs, operated by the 89th Airlift Wing.

The C-20C, three of which serve at Andrews (Air Force serials 85-0049, 85-0050, and 86-0403), is an emergency war-order aircraft designed to move high-ranking personnel quickly in the event of nuclear conflict, and carries hardened, strategic communications equipment. The C-20C lacks the digital "glass" cockpit found on modern jets. Instead, it has analogue instruments (round dials) that have changed little since the earliest days of aviation. The reason for the mechanical, rather than electronic, instruments is that the older gauges are invulnerable to EMP (electromagnetic pulse), the blast of energy that comes from a nuclear detonation and can fry anything that relies on electricity.

The Air Force has not disclosed details regarding the defensive system in the tail cone of the C-20C, which appears similar to systems on Air Force One and on the VC-137C. The system appears to be the one known as ISDS (IRCM Self-Defense System), also known as AN/APQ-17 "Have Siren." This is designed to defend from attack from the rear hemisphere by infrared (IR) guided missiles, primarily of the shoulder-fired type (which home-in on engine exhausts). IR signals are emitted by the device, confusing and overloading the seeker head of an attacking missile, causing it to lose lock on the intended target. The C-20C has one such ISDS device in an aft fairing under the tailfin. The E-3, Air Force One, and C-137s use ISDS, as do some fixed wing turboprops and other jets. 150 units had been delivered as of mid-2001.

The pilots and communications operators on the hush-hush C-20Cs are the same people who fly very prosaic and public Gulfstreams (C-20B and C-20H executive transports), but the C-20C version is a closely-guarded secret. Although public documents are available showing when they were built, fitted out, and delivered (in the late 1980s), nothing has ever appeared in public about their purpose. When asked about the C-20C, officials said, "Our position is that we do not have any aircraft called a C-20C" (an Air Force Materiel Command program manager at Wright-Patterson Air Force Base, Ohio), or "No comment" (a communications operator at Andrews), or "You will have to ask somebody else" (a Gulfstream pilot). When the author of this volume requested information about the C-20C from Brigadier General Ron Rand, the Air Force's chief of public affairs, officials responded months later saying they would be unable to help. The following is informed speculation, based on conversations with crews who discussed the hush-hush C-20C—but only a little.

Behind the curtain of secrecy is a program to assure the survival of government leaders in the midst of a nuclear attack. The program is euphemistically referred to as the "Senex" program (derived from "senior executives"), and the C-20Cs are sometimes called "Senex airplanes." Over the years, other terms applying to these aircraft have included the acronyms COOP (Continuity of [Government] Operations Program), COG (Continuity of Government), and PSSS (Presidential Successor Support System). These terms apparently apply not only to the mission of the C-20C but to war readiness efforts in various locations around Washington, including a now-defunct alternate underground facility for Congress in Greenbriar, West Virginia (abandoned after it was publicly revealed a few years ago) and an alternate National Military Command Center near Camp David, Maryland.

Apart from the presidential travel so familiar to the public, both Air Force One and the C-20C Gulfstream III have two additional presidential functions. The first function is to assure the survival of the National Command Authority, or NMC. Widely used incorrectly to refer to U.S. military command arrangements, the term NMC actually has a simpler meaning. It refers to the two officials authorized to release nuclear weapons—the president and the secretary of defense. The second function is to assure the survival of those in line for succession to the presidency, including the vice president, the Speaker of the House of Representatives, and the president pro tem of the Senate.

Whenever the president or secretary of defense travel, a C-20C Gulfstream IV always shadows their aircraft. If the president lands in Air Force One at, say, London's Heathrow International Airport, a C-20C will land at nearby Royal Air Force Northolt and remain on runway alert. Although it is clearly intended as backup transportation and as a source of communications support, an exact description of the C-20C's function remains elusive. When at home at Andrews, the C-20Cs have a special hangar near the hangar for Air Force One, and are rarely out-of-doors except when flying.

The C-20C is powered by two 11,400-pound Rolls-Royce F113-RR-100 (Spey Mk.511-8) turbofan engines. Because so little has been published about them, details on the three individual C-20Cs, beginning with the aircraft numbers assigned by their builder, appear below:

All three aircraft (456, 458, 473) were delivered "green" for outfitting with special mission equipment.

456 C-20C USAF 85-0050: Delivered March 15, 1985, to the 89th Military Airlift Wing at Andrews Air Force Base, Maryland. Fitted by E Systems. Now with 99thAS/89th AW.

458 C-20C USAF 85-0049: Delivered March 28, 1985, to the 89th Military Airlift Wing at Andrews Air Force Base, Maryland. Fitted by E Systems. Now with 99thAS/89th AW.

473 C-20C USAF 86-0403. Delivered December 27, 1985, to 89th Military Airlift Wing at Andrews Air Force Base, Maryland. Fitted at E Systems. Now with 99thAS/89th AW. Observed in August 1991 at Shannon in overall gloss white with same cheat line as SAM C-20, gold with blue outline, white color wraps under nose and to back of aircraft, under engines. Underside is highly polished silver metal. Observed April 30, 1992, at Andrews in same scheme.

The flat-ended, rounded fairing at the fuselage tail cone contains the C-20C's defensive system against infrared missiles, which may be designated AN/APR-17 "Have Siren." The probe sticking back from the rear fuselage is a high-frequency radio antenna. The aircraft also has a Satcom (satellite communication) antenna atop the fuselage at the point of the wing roots. All window shades on the C-20C are drawn.
John Gourley

VC-25A as viewed from above. *USAF*

buses began to decline. Those on the airlines began to skyrocket. It was size that mattered, not speed. The idea of an American supersonic transport did not last beyond 1970, but the concept of a huge aircraft, able to carry an unprecedented number of people, remains alive today.

The version of the 747 with the highest-density seating on today's airline routes carries up to 624 people. The 747 assigned to carry the president of the United States exists for only one passenger, often carries as few as two dozen, and rarely carries more than 60 people.

Although airliners with two engines and a two-person flight crew routinely circle the globe today, Air Force One was ordered at a time when the Pentagon's

Air Staff insisted that any plane carrying the president must have four engines and a four-person flight crew (pilot, co-pilot, navigator, and flight engineer). So, the Air Force One pilots have plenty of help, but their job is crucial and the system allows them no room for mistakes.

PRE-FLIGHT BRIEFING

Long before the president heads for Andrews to begin his trip, the AC, or aircraft commander (that is, the pilot in command), gathers the entire flight crew, including communication operators and flight attendants, around a conference table in the Presidential Airlift Group (formerly the Presidential Pilot's Office). Using charts and maps, the aircraft

VC-25A as viewed from beneath. Both leading- and trailing-edge flaps are deployed, and the landing gear apparently has been fully retracted only seconds earlier. First-time viewers often remark on the pristine appearance of the aircraft, which is kept in like-new condition by a cadre of maintenance personnel who qualify for their job only after a personal interview. *Jim Kippen*

commander informs everyone where they're going and how they'll get there. Then, the AC turns the floor over to an intelligence officer who briefs the crew on their destination. It may be Chicago, and this portion of the briefing may consist of nothing more than a description of a hotel. Or the destination may be Vilnius, Lithuania, and the intelligence briefing will include the prospects of being robbed by a pickpocket or attacked by terrorists.

The intelligence officer who, as of this writing, provides the intelligence briefing to the crew is First Lieutenant Nathan Jones, who probably needs to know about more different subjects than anyone else in the Air Force. Jones' knowledge ranges from the performance of Russian-built MiG fighters to the personality of the Lithuanian prime minister. Unlike the rest of the crew of Air Force One, Jones has access to "all source intelligence," meaning that he is cleared for the information that results from communications intelligence and satellite reconnaissance. Contrary to myth, Air Force One is almost never escorted by friendly fighters—but Jones must tell the crew whether anybody else's fighters will be in the area.

Jones' briefing will range from a few minutes to an hour, depending on the destination, the level of threat (if any) confronting Air Force One, and the amount of intelligence available on the mission. It should be emphasized that the president's security, and intelligence related to it, remains the job of the Secret Service and is handled separately from the preparations by the crew of Air Force One for their mission.

After the intelligence brief, the aircraft commander runs over the flight plan. At this juncture, the airborne communications systems operator (ACSO) reviews the communication needs for the flight. It would be impossible to exaggerate the importance of the ACSO—still, in everyday conversation, called a "radio operator"—to the mission of the 747.

Air Force One has crew positions for three ACSOs and almost always carries a fourth in reserve. The communications center is located in the stretched upper deck of the aircraft, used on the airline version to carry passengers. Today aboard Air Force One the ACSO will operate radios, but he must also enable the president and other passengers

When the 757-200 was chosen over the 767-200 for the C-32A mission—including frequent duty hauling the vice president as Air Force Two—the Air Force released this artist's conception of what the new aircraft would look like. By the time the builder delivered the C-32A in 1998, the paint scheme on the aircraft had changed significantly. The black anti-glare panels on the nose gave way to an extension of the blue color on the lower fuselage. *Boeing*

Although the C-32A has been part of the 89th Airlift Wing since 1998, it is not usually used for presidential travel. In fact, when this volume went to press in 2002, the C-32A had carried the chief executive only once—during one of President George W. Bush's first trips in office.

The C-32A is a specially configured version of the Boeing 757-200 commercial intercontinental airliner. The primary customers are the vice president (using the call sign Air Force Two), the first lady, and members of the Cabinet and Congress. The C-32 replaces the C-137 aircraft. Active-duty aircrews from the 89th Wing's 1st Airlift Squadron fly the aircraft.

The C-32A body is identical to that of the Boeing 757-200, but has different interior furnishings and avionics.

The passenger cabin is divided into four sections: The forward area has a communications center, galley, lavatory and 10 business class seats. The second section is a fully enclosed stateroom for the use of the primary passenger. It includes a changing area, private lavatory, separate entertainment system, two first-class swivel seats and a convertible divan that seats three and folds out to a bed. The third section contains the conference and staff facility with eight business class seats. The rear section of the cabin contains general seating with 32 business-class seats, galley, two lavatories, and closets.

In a curious comment on the aircraft, an Air Force press release tells us, "Because the C-32A is a high-standing aircraft, it is easier to see under and around it—an important security factor for protecting the plane and its passengers." The same release says that the C-32A "is more fuel efficient and has improved capabilities over its C-137 predecessor."

Well, almost. When the C-32A first reported on duty, the Air Force was embarrassed that it had shorter range than the ancient C-137. Range is an all-important consideration for people who travel frequently to Europe and do not want to stop on the way. The Air Force solved the problem by arranging to have Boeing Wichita install internal fuselage fuel tanks that increase range but reduce fuselage space. After the modifications, the C-32A's 92,000-pound fuel capacity allows the aircraft to travel 5,500 nautical miles unrefueled.

Compared to the C-137, the C-32A can operate on shorter runways down to 5,000 feet in length. The C-32A is equipped with TCAS (Traffic Collision Avoidance System) that gives advance warning of possible air crashes. Other items include a typical, modern-day navigation system with GPS (Global Positioning System) and a Flight Management System/Electronic Flight Instrument System. Inside the C-32A, communications are paramount.

Boeing rolled out the first C-32A VIP transport in Seattle on January 30, 1998. The aircraft made its maiden flight from Renton Municipal Airport on February 11.

The USAF is employing commercial purchase procedures to buy four C-32A (Boeing 757-200) transports (98-0001/0004) plus two C-37As (Gulfstream V) (97-0400/0401). They will replace the Air Force's aging fleet of C-137B/C (Boeing 707-320B) transports, which once numbered seven aircraft and was down to one in 2001. Plans to lease some or all of the new aircraft have been set aside. The mix of 757s and G-Vs was chosen after the Air Staff decided that it would be too ostentatious to purchase four Boeing 767s, the aircraft that was originally designated C-32. In retrospect, many airmen believe the more capable 767 would have been a smart purchase.

The first of the four C-32As reached Andrews in 1998 following several delays that made the aircraft enter service about a year later than once planned. The Air Force has a fifth 757-200 that is unmarked and is used to transport special operations personnel.

C-32A SPECIFICATIONS

Powerplants: four Pratt and Whitney 2040 engines rated at 41,700 pounds static thrust per engine

Wingspan: 124 feet 8 inches

Length: 155 feet 3 inches

Height: 44 feet 6 inches

Maximum takeoff weight: 255,000 pounds

Range: 5,500 nautical miles

Ceiling: 42,000 feet

Speed: 530 miles per hour

Load: 45 passengers

Crew: 16

The first C-32A rolls out of the factory in on January 30, 1998. Three and one-half years later, the C-32A had only carried the president (and earned the call sign Air Force One) on a single occasion. But the aircraft carries other government officials regularly. According to the builder, the paint scheme, inspired by the color design on the presidential VC-25A, required 85 gallons of paint. *Boeing*

The first C-32A (98-0001) at Andrews Air Force Base on October 28, 1998, shortly after delivery and before being modified with internal fuselage fuel tanks to improve range. Often employed to carry the vice president as Air Force Two, the C-32A also served frequently as a backup to the VC-25A. *Robert F. Dorr*

The second C-32A (98-0002) at Andrews on March 19, 1999, with a pair of UH-1H Huey helicopters of the 89th Wing's 1st Helicopter Squadron prancing past in the background. On this date, the C-32A was providing transportation for First Lady Hillary Rodham Clinton. The president's spouse does not warrant the Air Force One call sign: a mission hauling the first lady is known as a "Phoenix Copper" flight. *Robert F. Dorr*

The second VC-25A built for presidential travel, SAM 29000, waits at Barksdale Air Force Base, Louisiana, with its self-contained "air stairs" deployed and an Air Force Security Forces automobile parked alongside. The resplendent colors of the aircraft are a testimony to hard work by enlisted airmen of the 89th Airlift Wing, who take enormous pride in supporting the chief executive's airplane and strive to keep it immaculate. *Greg L. Davis*

With a fuselage length of 231 feet 10 inches, the president's Boeing 747-200B can hardly be kept hidden when out-of-doors. VC-25A 86-28000 was at the south end of Andrews Air Force Base, perhaps a quarter mile from its assigned hangar, on December 18, 1997. By coincidence, that week, the 89th Airlift Wing commander at the time, Brigadier General Arthur J. Lichte, sent a memorandum reminding troops that airplanes at Andrews belong to the American people, and lifting all restrictions on exterior photography of aircraft assigned to the 89th. *Robert F. Dorr*

to use telephones, e-mail, and movies. After briefing with the crew, the ACSO will also brief with the Secret Service. While Air Force One is in flight, the ACSO will be the eyes and ears of the super-secret White House Communications Agency, which keeps the president in touch and ready for almost any crisis.

Like the other crew members, Air Force One's flight attendants have also been preparing. Flight attendants begin planning 48 hours prior to a presidential mission. From one end of the resplendent blue-and-white VC-25A to the other, the flight attendants are responsible for the cleanliness and orderly functioning of 4,000 square feet of cabin space. While the flight is being planned, they stock groceries (purchased anonymously at a constantly shifting roster of retail outlets near Andrews), spruce up furnishings and furniture, and even make the president's bed. There are two presidential bunks and one is always kept ready for the chief

executive to recline, should he choose. As one flight attendant told the author, "Whether it's a day trip or a summit trip, everything must work right."

DEPARTURE

Pilots, flight crew, and the remainder of Air Force One's crew are inside the airplane, buttoned up, preparing to go, long before the chief executive's motorcade arrives. The last step consists of the aircraft commander and co-pilot running through the before-start checklist, with one uttering the "challenge" (in the tone of voice of a question) and the other giving the "response." Samples:

Q: Departure briefing?

A: *Complete*

Q: FMCs [flight management systems], radios?

A: *Programmed, set, verified.*

Q: IRSs [inertial reference systems]?

A: *Nav [navigation] aligned.*

Q: Hydraulic demand pumps?

A: No. 1 auto, no. 4 aux [auxiliary]

Q: Oil quantity?

A: Normal.

The pilots inform the crew and those monitoring their preparations from outside the aircraft that they are ready to take off. They obtain clearance to taxi. The pilots receive a "block time" for departure. They will attempt to meet that deadline within ten seconds. Usually, everything goes like clockwork.

But first, they wait.

The last person aboard before the president is a military officer (Air Force, Army, or Marine Corps colonel, or Coast Guard or Navy captain) carrying the "football," the package containing the codes that enable the president to launch a nuclear strike. The protocol that places the "football" so close to the president and gives the device its name has solidified into ritual. By law, only the president or the secretary of defense can authorize the release of nuclear weapons. The device is simply a large briefcase, and the job is rotated with punctilio among officers of the five military service branches, but parlance requires that it be called the "football" and nothing else.

If the president's party arrives at Air Force One on time, he and his fellow travelers come aboard exactly as the pilots complete their before-flight checklist. Air Force One's tires will begin to turn, almost always, exactly at "block time." Otherwise, the pilots and crew will wait on their passengers. It is the opposite of what happens on the airlines. Because of his importance, and also for security reasons, the boarding of the president is the last thing that happens before Air Force One begins to roll.

Air Force One taxies much faster than airliners usually do, its crew secure in the knowledge that no aircraft or vehicle will be in their way. The pilot in command obtains takeoff clearance while rolling, and the two pilots complete the before-takeoff checklist while in motion. Most of the time, the VC-25A rounds the turn onto the active runway and begins its takeoff roll without hesitation. With the enormous power of its two engines unleashed—

the equivalent of two railway locomotives, or enough thrust to propel the VC-25A straight up—the mighty aircraft lifts into the sky and begins its flight, the airways ahead being cleared as it climbs.

Before the president's aircraft departs, a fleet of other aircraft are already well on the way, or at the destination, with necessary travel items. Almost always, a presidential limousine goes with the president, carried by an Air Force cargo plane. A duplicate limousine and Secret Service vehicles are also carried to the destination by Air Force cargo planes. Everything will be in place when the chief executive arrives.

ON ARRIVAL

Speed—not haste, but measured, prudent, and deliberate speed—is a factor in the operations of Air Force One at all times. A high-speed taxi is often vital to the plan for the day, not only on departure but on arrival as well. When President Ronald Reagan lay on the operating table after being shot by a would-be assassin on March 30, 1981, Air Force Two happened to be bringing Vice President George Bush home from a trip. No one knew whether there was a further threat to U.S. leaders or whether, at any instant, Reagan might die, making Bush president. Bush's plane taxied at a rapid pace into the hangar, and the vice president did not emerge from the aircraft until the hangar had been shut down and the aircraft surrounded by security.

Even a landing in normal times triggers a ritual of activity. The military officer with the football hits the ground first and hands off his precious package to his successor. The president prepares to face his public, inevitably before a microphone. When he steps down from the aircraft, a general or colonel greets him at the steps. If the arrival site is Andrews, the greeter is usually the 89th Wing commander.

PROPELLERS FOR THE PRESIDENT

Theodore Roosevelt may have been the most adventurous American president. The man who led his Rough Riders in the courageous charge at Cuba's San Juan Heights during the Spanish-American War continued to show his audacious nature by seeking out friendship with Wilbur and Orville Wright. He encouraged the pioneering brothers by proclaiming that the airplane "has a great future."

While participating in the Missouri State Republican campaign in St. Louis, Missouri, on October 11, 1910, Roosevelt was invited to fly in a Wright Type B biplane with pilot Arch Hoxsey. As the 26th president from 1901 to 1909, Roosevelt was not in office when he made the flight, but by sitting in a shuddering biplane made of wood and fabric, he defied the accepted wisdom of what was safe for a president and what was not. Critics said that Roosevelt was too adventurous, that he was pushing things too far.

This Boeing 314 Clipper, bearing civil registry NC18609, was named the *Pacific Clipper*. Operated by a Navy crew for Pan American Airways during the war, it was known in Navy jargon as B-314, bureau no. 48228. This ship was built immediately after NC18606, the identical flying boat named the *Dixie Clipper* that carried President Franklin D. Roosevelt to Casablanca. *Harold G. Martin*

There exists surviving motion picture footage of Roosevelt arriving at the Kinloch aviation field accompanied by Governor Herbert S. Hadley of Missouri, entering the passenger seat, flying, and descending to join his waiting party. Roosevelt later commented to a *New York Times* reporter, "You know I didn't intend to do it, but when I saw the thing there, I could not resist it." No man was a better candidate to become the first president to fly.

Roosevelt's successors as chief executive—William Howard Taft (1909–1913), Woodrow Wilson (1913–1921), Warren Harding (1921–1923), Calvin Coolidge (1923–1929), and Herbert Hoover (1929–1933)—walked, rode in automobiles, or took the train while in office. There is no record, in fact, that any of these men flew in an aircraft while they served as president of the United States, although Hoover certainly did so after leaving office.

Before he became the 32nd president (1933–1945), Franklin D. Roosevelt had several occasions to fly. The most famous occurred in July 1932 when, already chosen as his party's nominee for the presidency, FDR flew from Albany, New York, to Chicago, Illinois, to attend the Democratic convention in an American Airways, Inc., Ford Tri-Motor registered as NC415H. With its mostly-metal structure and corrugated fuselage skin, the ungainly Tri-Motor was known as the "Tin Lizzie," but the name was meant affectionately. It was a reliable flying machine and performed its duty for FDR without a hitch.

FDR eventually became the first president to fly while in office. It was during the time of World War II. Many in the press and public still regarded aviation as dangerous, but there was no rule, written or unwritten, against the chief executive flying in an aircraft. The world was on the brink of change.

THREE PLANES MEANT FOR FDR

There is evidence that a Navy Douglas RD-2 Dolphin was assigned to presidential support duties in 1936 during FDR's time in office. The nation's ad-

mirals may have seen that presidential air travel was inevitable, and may have had in mind launching an early bid to land the job of carrying the chief executive.

No prettier than the Ford Tri-Motor but as practical as they came, the Dolphin was a popular, high-wing, twin-engined monoplane amphibian powered by two 350-horsepower Wright R-975-3 radial piston engines and capable of a maximum speed of 140 miles per hour. It was a popular aircraft in the 1930s with the Army, Navy, and Coast Guard.

RD-2 Dolphin bureau no. 9347 was the subject of a letter from the commander of Naval Air Station Anacostia in Washington, D.C. to the chief of the Navy's Bureau of Aeronautics, reading in part: "Although not exclusively used for the President and the Sec[retary] of the Navy, this plane was set aside to carry the mail to the President when he was embarked in the Potomac [River, aboard the presidential yacht] and it was used by the Assistant Sec[retary] of the Navy, the late Colonel H. L. Roosevelt, for official transportation. It is very necessary to have a plane of this type on this station at all times for transportation of mail and guests of the President."

Navy records are ambiguous as to whether the service ever intended the Dolphin specifically to carry the chief executive. Undoubtedly, the Navy must have hoped it would receive the honor of transporting the president. If the Dolphin was intended in part for that purpose, it became the first aircraft ever to draw such an assignment—but the president never flew in it.

Additionally, a Curtiss YC-30 Condor twin-engined biplane stationed at Bolling Field in Washington, D.C., in the late 1930s was believed by many to be earmarked as a presidential aircraft. No record confirming this has ever been found, and Roosevelt did not fly in the Condor, either.

Lastly, the *Guess Where II*, a transport version of the Consolidated B-24D Liberator four-engined heavy bomber known as a C-87A, was assigned for presidential travel for a period of more than one year.

During this time, it completed several extensive trips. One of these was a round-the-world journey begun on July 25, 1943, carrying five senators on what would be known today as a fact-finding tour. *Guess Where II* also carried First Lady Eleanor Roosevelt—but never her husband. Army Air Forces flyers were severely disappointed that their plans to transport the boss in the C-87A never materialized.

FIRST PRESIDENTIAL FLIGHT

Despite the objections of many in the Secret Service and in the Executive Mansion, Roosevelt mustered his great sense of historical drama and used it to fly from Miami, Florida, to Casablanca, Morocco, in January 1943 to attend a meeting with Prime Minister Winston Churchill and other Allied leaders to plot Allied strategy for the war. Although plans were forming for a military squadron to transport the president by air, Roosevelt found himself journeying aboard a civilian plane. The Secret Service had

ruled out travel by sea, leery of the threat from German submarines. But the protectors of the chief executive felt little happiness about Roosevelt flying.

The attitude of at least one observer was summed up by columnist Christopher Wayne of the *Washington, D.C., Evening Star*, who wrote in a January 1943 editorial piece that "Aviation is demanding and unforgiving. It is still not clear that the obvious advantages of air travel carry greater weight than the peril incurred by risking the life of a president on a journey through the sky."

Flying Boat Trip

Roosevelt took off from Dinner Key Seaplane Base in Miami on January 11, 1943, as a passenger in a Boeing 314 Clipper. The aircraft wore the civil registry number NC18605 and was named the *Dixie Clipper*. The plane was also assigned the U.S. Navy bureau number 48226 and constructor's number 1992.

Seen here in San Francisco Bay, with Treasure Island in the background, is one of four flying boats that were given the Army Air Forces' designation C-98, even though they were among a dozen similar planes operated by a Navy crew for Pan American Airways. This aircraft, registered as NC18612 and assigned Army serial 42-88622 (and simultaneously, Navy bureau no. 99081), was a sister ship to the aircraft Roosevelt used for his Casablanca meeting with Churchill. *Boeing*

Eleanor Roosevelt stands in the center of a throng of military and civilian officials in front of *Guess Where II*, the C-87A Liberator Express tailored for presidential use but never flown by a president. The occasion is a trip to Central and South America by the first lady in March 1944. *AAF via Robert C. Mikesh*

The distinction of being the first aircraft customized for presidential travel belongs to the military transport version of the Consolidated B-24D Liberator four-engined heavy bomber. On June 2, 1943, this C-87A Liberator Express (41-24159) was accepted by the 503rd Army Air Base Unit at Washington, D.C., National Airport. The first presidential pilot, Major (later Colonel) Henry T. "Hank" Myers, dubbed the unit the "Brass Hat Squadron" and named the aircraft *Guess Where II*. An important consideration in the choice of aircraft was long range, to avoid the security problems that might arise with frequent stopovers. The C-87A offered the rather extraordinary range of 2,900 miles.

According to retired Major Robert C. Mikesh, the leading authority on presidential aircraft, Myers intended the name of the C-87A to be a word play on the question, "Guess where to?" There was never an air-

craft named *Guess Where I*. It is a myth that the name came from Roosevelt and related to his famous quote about the April 1942 bombing raid on Japan by Lieutenant Colonel James Doolittle's B-25 Mitchell raiders. The B-25s had taken off from an aircraft carrier in the western Pacific, but when Roosevelt was asked their point of departure, he first challenged a reporter to, "Guess where," then replied with alacrity, "Shangri-la." The latter was the fictitious oriental redoubt in James Hilton's novel *Lost Horizon*; it was the president's way of saying that the reporters could keep right on guessing.

Wearing standard Army olive-drab paint with a light gray underside, *Guess Where II* boasted four compartments similar to the sleeper compartments of railroad trains of the era. It could accommodate nine VIP passengers with overnight sleeping arrangements or 20

passengers by day. The C-87A also had two lavatories and a full galley.

The Army acquired 280 C-87 and five C-87A models for transport duty, all built by Consolidated in Fort Worth, Texas. All were powered by four 1,200-horsepower Pratt & Whitney R-1830-43 Twin Wasp 18-cylinder turbocharged radial piston engines. All had a cruising speed of 200 miles per hour and could probably work their way up to 290 miles per hour for brief periods under the right conditions. Air Transport Command pilot Ernest K. Gann was one of many who was not enthusiastic about these transports made from bombers. "The assembly of parts known collectively as a C-87 will never replace the airplane," Gann opined. "They were an evil, bastard contraption, nothing like the relatively efficient B-24 except in appearance . . . the C-87s could not carry enough ice to chill a highball."

Apparently, *Guess Where II* was ready by the time Roosevelt made his second overseas trip in November 1943 to meet Britain's Prime Minister Winston Churchill and the Soviet Union's Premier Josef Stalin at

Tehran and Cairo. But Myers, the C-87A, and the presidential crew were not tapped for the job. Reportedly, the Secret Service had a view of the C-87A not dissimilar to Gann's. "A firetrap," one critic is supposed to have argued. As recounted in the accompanying text, Roosevelt flew a different aircraft on the journey.

The Secret Service and the Army never permitted *Guess Where II* to perform the presidential mission for which it had been built. Nevertheless, serving with the Brass Hats (forerunners of today's 89th Airlift Wing), the C-87A carried senior military and government officials on numerous trips. Apparently, safety concerns for the first lady were less stringent, for the C-87A carried Eleanor Roosevelt on a March 1944 tour of American military installations in the Caribbean and Latin America.

Guess Where II continued to haul dignitaries until its final flight on October 30, 1945, when its destination was Walnut Ridge, Arkansas. Here, the first plane designed for a president—which never carried a president—was ignominiously retired and later scrapped.

The presidential C-87A Liberator Express, *Guess Where II. AAF via Robert C. Mikesh*

Roosevelt traveled on the presidential rail car, the *Ferdinand Magellan*, from Washington, D.C., to Miami, where he boarded the 314 Clipper, a long-range, four-engine flying boat used for trans-Atlantic flights before World War II. For the president's comfort, a double bed was installed. The huge flying boat was one of several operated for the Navy by Pan American Airways (known as PAA; the nickname Pan Am still lay in the future). Lieutenant Howard M. Cone of the U.S. Navy Reserve was the pilot during this first presidential flight.

At the time, it was not only controversial for a president to fly, it was also controversial for a president to leave American soil. None had previously done so during wartime, and no president since Abraham Lincoln had ever traveled to a war zone.

Roosevelt's flying trip was enough to test anyone's stamina. With eight other passengers accompanying the president, pilot Cone embarked on a journey consisting of three segments, beginning with a 1,633-mile flight to Port of Spain, Trinidad. The next day, the silvery, triple-tailed Clipper continued on a 1,227-mile leg for Belém, Brazil, covering the distance in about eight hours. The following day, the Clipper piloted by Cone flew the longest leg of this expedition, covering the 2,500 miles to Bathurst, British Gambia, in West Africa (known today as Banjul, Gambia).

Presidential Plane No. 2

On the heels of Clipper pilot Cone, the second pilot to provide transportation to Roosevelt was Otis F. Bryan, a major in the Army Reserve and a vice president of Trans-World Airlines. Bryan was waiting in Bathurst with a Douglas C-54 Skymaster, which was operated by TWA under a wartime contract to the government.

As a C-54 passenger, Roosevelt flew 1,500 miles to Casablanca and to one of several crucial conferences with Allied leaders. He arrived on January 14, 1943. After spending a fortnight in North Africa, Roosevelt returned to Washington by retracing his path aboard the same two aircraft.

As noted in the sidebar on the previous page, Roosevelt traveled to conferences in Tehran and Cairo in November 1943 aboard another TWA C-54 Skymaster, rather than using the C-87A Liberator Express named *Guess Where II* that had been built for his use. The C-87A never carried a president, and Roosevelt's own, personal C-54 did not become available until eight months after the November 1943 meetings.

This record of presidential travel has often proven confusing to those who try to write about it today. It is important to remember that Roosevelt was blazing a trail. Once he established a precedent by demonstrating that the occupant of the White House could travel abroad and fly in aircraft, it was never seriously questioned again. A few recalcitrant taxpayers undoubtedly still believe, even in the twenty-first century, that their dollars would be better spent keeping the president at work in his office. Some certainly would argue that he could travel a little less ostentatiously than he does today. But after Roosevelt, aerial travel by presidents became the norm.

A NEW AIRCRAFT

On June 12, 1944, pilot Major Henry T. "Hank" Myers traveled to the Douglas Aircraft plant in Santa Monica, California. Myers' mission was to pick up a new C-54 Skymaster transport and deliver it to Washington National Airport, where it would be assigned to the 503rd Army Air Base Unit of the Air Transport Command. The unit was a precursor of today's 89th Airlift Wing, Air Mobility Command, and was a part of the Army Air Forces, the predecessor of today's Air Force.

The C-54 to all appearances was a routine, four-engined transport designed for long-range flying, one of a new generation of planes able to span vast stretches of ocean with very few refueling stops. But Myers' C-54 was special. It was the first transport designed and built to be a presidential airplane. The term "Air Force One" did not yet exist, and C-54C no. 42-107451 was known at first simply as "Project 51" and later as the "Flying

White House." Most in Washington referred to Franklin D. Roosevelt's personal plane by the informal name it had been given, the *Sacred Cow*.

Retired Major Robert C. Mikesh, an authority on presidential aircraft, describes the way the *Sacred Cow* had been tailored to Roosevelt's needs: "[The] most unique feature of this aircraft was that it contained a battery-operated elevator, located aft of the main passenger cabin, which could lift a passenger directly from the ground to the cabin-level floor. This elevator represented a security measure as well as a convenience. The president's need to walk with crutches or use a wheelchair was an important factor in developing 'Project 51.' In the past, it had been necessary to construct bulky ramps to aid Mr. Roosevelt in embarking or debarking from an airplane. The very presence of such ramps at a foreign airfield suggested the impending arrival of FDR. Advance notification of the president as an incoming passenger was, of course, undesirable during World War II. The elevator eliminated the need for telltale ramps."

The aircraft had a bullet-proof picture window. A 7.5x12-foot stateroom occupied the aft portion of the cabin, providing seating for seven. Included was a sofa that opened electrically into a bed, two

electrically folding chairs, and a full galley. In addition to pilot Myers, a crew of six manned the airplane. Myers' co-pilot was Captain Elmer Smith, who later retired as colonel. The stewards (who would be called flight attendants in today's Air Force jargon) were nicknamed "hotcuppers" because they were equipped with electric hotcup devices to heat coffee and soup—"not very luxurious by today's standards," according to former flight attendant John Haigh.

The interior of Roosevelt's C-54 was furnished with upholstery of blue wool. Draperies at the win-

The *Sacred Cow* following its arrival at the Air Force Museum at Wright-Patterson Air Force Base in Dayton, Ohio. After retirement from a long career of worldwide travels, only some of which were presidential, the *Sacred Cow* was given to the National Air Museum in Washington, D.C. In a move that some consider controversial, that museum then gave the C-54C to the museum in Dayton. *David W. Menard*

dows were of blue gabardine, on which was embroidered the insignia of the Army, Navy, Marine Corps, and Coast Guard. The aircraft was provided with its own set of dishes, silverware, and other amenities.

The *Sacred Cow* had been built for presidential use in part because the Secret Service felt the German U-boat threat made it unsafe for the chief executive to travel by sea across the Atlantic. Roosevelt, following his earlier trips on a Boeing 314 Clipper and a stock C-54, used the *Sacred Cow* for only one overseas trip, but it was his most important.

TRAVEL ON THE SACRED COW

Crossing the Atlantic aboard the heavy cruiser *Quincy*, the president arrived on the island of Malta. On February 3, 1945, he boarded the *Sacred Cow* for a trip to Yalta in the Soviet Union. He met with Britain's Winston Churchill and Russia's Josef Stalin until February 12. It was the first summit conference among the three leaders to discuss Allied strategy. Roosevelt then re-boarded the *Sacred Cow* for a flight to Cairo, Egypt, where he rejoined the *Quincy* for the trip home.

When Roosevelt died on April 12, 1945, the *Sacred Cow* became President Harry S. Truman's aircraft. As the 33rd president (1945–1953), Truman became the first chief executive to fly on a regular basis. He used the *Sacred Cow* to travel to Kansas City on his way to visit his hometown of Independence, Missouri. This was the first domestic air trip by a president while in office.

The *Sacred Cow* performed White House duty until 1947. Even after it was no longer a flying White House, the *Sacred Cow* soldiered on. Retired Colonel Ancil Baker was one of many who flew the C-54 extensively from 1948 to 1963, after it was no longer employed for presidential travel.

Colonel Baker recalls, "The *Sacred Cow* was turned over to Headquarters Command, U.S. Air Force at Bolling Air Force Base in Washington, D.C. I flew it quite a bit. I took it to Mexico City, Ottawa, Goose Bay, Iceland, Wiesbaden, Copenhagen, Paris, Madrid, Lajes, and Puerto Rico. We carried the Air Force band around.

"Our crew consisted of pilot, co-pilot, and flight engineer. We had no radio operator and no steward. The aircraft still had an elevator, a private

room for the president, an overstuffed chair with an oversized window, and a desk. On the wall facing the president's desk was a huge seascape—Roosevelt having been a naval person all his life. There was a bed on one side of the office and a passageway on the right. The aircraft still had Roosevelt's elevator. We used the elevator to store cheap foreign liquor that we brought home from overseas."

Later, Baker saw the *Sacred Cow* again "in bits and pieces" at the Air Force Museum in Dayton, Ohio, where it is displayed intact today. "They were replacing the Douglas [Aircraft Company] emblem on the control yoke, so they gave me the original."

In 1947, the *Sacred Cow* was replaced for presidential travel by a C-118 named the *Independence*, also piloted by Lieutenant Colonel Henry T. "Hank" Myers. On December 4, 1961, Major General Brooke E. Allen, commander of the Air Force's Headquarters Command in Washington carried out the transfer of the *Sacred Cow* to the National Air Museum, predecessor of today's National Air and Space Museum. Subsequently, the museum released the aircraft for further transfer to the Air Force Museum at Wright-Patterson Air

Seen on August 5, 1948, when it was no longer a presidential aircraft, the *Sacred Cow* now had a red stripe inside the bar on its U.S. national insignia, a change adopted for all U.S. military aircraft the previous year. *USAF via Jim Kippen*

Force Base near Dayton, Ohio. Museum experts studying the plane have discovered that the *Sacred Cow* had a unique aileron configuration not found on other C-54s; as displayed today, the plane has a standard C-54 outer wing but all other parts are original.

INTRODUCING THE INDEPENDENCE

In 1946, the Army Air Forces made arrangements with Douglas Aircraft to acquire a production DC-6 airliner for executive use by the president.

The prototype for the DC-6 series began flight tests at the Santa Monica, California, factory on February 15, 1946. At this time, the DC-6 was the standard against which other airliners were measured. It was powered by four 2,100-horsepower Pratt & Whitney R-2800-34 Double Wasp CA15 engines, replacing the R-2000 Twin Wasp used on the DC-4. This was a proven engine with tens of thousands of hours of wartime experience in planes like the P-47 Thunderbolt and F4U Corsair. It was an 18-cylinder, twin-row radial, air-cooled engine with a single-stage, two-speed integral supercharger. The version of the DC-6 that became President Truman's *Independence* also became the first American military transport to use and test reversible-pitch propellers, as well as the first with water injection in the engine for added thrust on takeoff. The presidential airplane had greater fuel capacity than the standard DC-6, enough for an absolute range of 4,400 miles.

The *Independence* was equipped with an experimental weather radar (the first in a DC-6), a radar altimeter, autopilot, and other advanced navigation equipment. With a cruising speed of 300 miles per hour and a normal range under standard operating conditions of 3,000 miles, the *Independence* could reach any location in the continental United States nonstop.

American Airlines relinquished the 29th position for a DC-6 on the production line to enable the Army to acquire an early aircraft, constructor's number 42881, and the Army assigned it the serial number 46-505 and the designation C-118. The

President Harry S. Truman's VC-118-DO was named *Independence*. It wore the Army Air Forces serial number 46-505 and was known to its manufacturer by constructor's number 42881. This color portrait shows the Independence after it reached the Air Force Museum at Wright-Patterson. *David W. Menard*

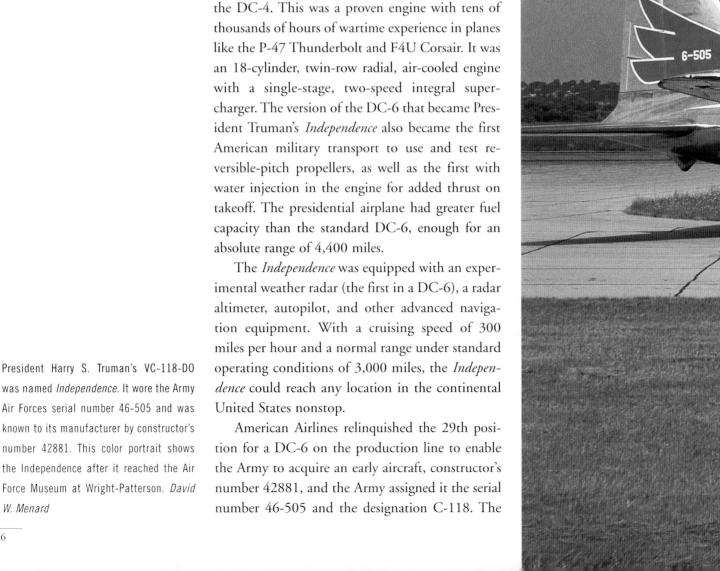

plane became the only C-118 ever to serve in the Air Force, although the service later acquired numerous DC-6A airplanes, designated C-118A.

The new plane for President Truman differed from civilian DC-6s because it had three closely grouped windows on the rear starboard side of the fuselage. This was the location of the presidential stateroom, entered through a bleached-mahogany door bearing the Great Seal of the United States. The room was decorated in chocolate brown, dark blue, and gray. The interior of the aircraft was configured to carry 25 passengers (compared with 52 in the airliner version). The main cabin could sleep 12 passengers.

Ever sensitive to perceptions, officials in Washington grimaced when an aviation magazine began calling the new plane the *Sacred Cow II*. Throughout

President Truman's C-118 Liftmaster, the *Independence*, while in service. *USAF via Jim Kippen*

the history of presidential air travel, officials would worry about the American taxpayer perceiving the chief executive's airplane as too glamorous or, worse, too ostentatious. To head off the unwanted name, Col. Myers chose the name *Independence*, which was the name of Truman's hometown in Missouri but also, in Myers' view, a name with a "national flavor."

On July 27, 1947, Truman was aboard the *Independence* when he affixed his signature to the National Security Act, which among other things established the U.S. Air Force as a separate military service branch, having equal footing with the Army, Coast Guard, Navy, and Marine Corps. The act also created the Department of Defense and the Central Intelligence Agency, but to those who served in the nation's military flying arm, the creation

of an independent Air Force was much welcomed, if long overdue.

On January 6, 1948, Colonel Francis T. Williams replaced Myers as the presidential pilot. Myers returned to his civilian job as a pilot with American Airlines. The two men began a long tradition of presidential pilots that continues today, in an era when the job has become more and more political. Since the 1980s, the authority and influence of the presidential pilot has varied according to the individual and the administration. What began as a prestigious but straightforward military assignment would eventually evolve into an assignment away from the mainstream of the military and close to the staff of the White House.

On June 1, 1948, a new Military Air Transport Service (MATS) replaced the former Air Transport Command. The unit operating presidential airplanes at Washington National Airport was established as the 1254th Air Transport Squadron on October 1, 1948, following the consolidation of several units. The presidential outfit would undergo several name changes before evolving into today's 89th Airlift Wing; at the time of its founding, it was commanded by Williams.

During the years when Truman continued to be an occasional flyer aboard the *Independence*, another change of military nomenclature took place. On August 1, 1952, the 1254th was redesignated a group, and two squadrons were established. The 1298th Air Transport Squadron was assigned responsibility for overseas missions with four-engined aircraft from Washington National. The 1299th Air Transport Squadron, soon to be equipped with twin-engined Convair transports, was located across the Potomac River at Bolling Air Force Base, D.C., for domestic missions carrying the president and other VIPs.

"Truman was not that much of an air traveler," remembers one officer who has followed the development of presidential travel. "Remember, during his era the railroad train was still the primary way of getting around. But he did make use of the *Independence* and he was respected and liked by those who flew him."

The Air Force chose wisely when it picked a military version of the Douglas DC-6 for President Harry S. Truman. The four-engined transport was a mature and sensible design offering speed, range, and comfort. This military DC-6 or C-118 Liftmaster shown here (53-3229) was operated by the presidential flying unit in the Washington, D.C., area but did not join the Air Force until 1954, the year after Truman left office. This aircraft served as a backup for the subsequent president, Dwight D. Eisenhower. Retired from the Air Force in 1975, this plane operated with a civilian user in Mexico before it finally was retired from flying duties in 1995. *Robert F. Dorr*

THE JET AGE

After World War II, Supreme Allied Commander in Europe Dwight D. Eisenhower traveled in a C-121A Constellation named *Columbine* (after the state flower of Colorado, the home state of Eisenhower's wife Mamie). After moving into the White House on January 20, 1953, Eisenhower selected as his personal aircraft another C-121A Constellation operated by the 1254th Air Transport Group at Washington National Airport. The plane was quickly dubbed *Columbine II.* The name was painted in flowery script across the nose of the aircraft above a likeness of a blue columbine. The presidential pilot, Air Force Colonel William G. "Bill" Draper, flew the aircraft, led the crew, and served Eisenhower as a kind of extra military advisor. Draper had also been Ike's pilot in Europe.

President Dwight D. Eisenhower selected as his personal aircraft this C-121A Constellation. The plane, pictured in 1953 with its crew, the 1254th Air Transport Group at Washington National Airport, was named *Columbine II.* The first *Columbine*, also a C-121A, carried General Eisenhower after the Second World War, and was named after the state flower of Colorado—his wife Mamie's home state. The *Columbine II,* with its distinctive triple tail, was powered by four Wright R-3350 (749C-18BD1) Cyclone piston engines with a combined 10,000 horsepower. The plane is currently on display at the Santa Fe Municipal Airport, Santa Fe, New Mexico. *Courtesy of the National Archives*

The original Lockheed C-121A Constellation *Columbine*. The Constellation was a military version of the commercial Lockheed Model 749, with strengthened floors and a cargo door to the port side of the rear fuselage. Many consider the Constellation and its kin to be the high point in propeller aircraft design. In addition to their military service, they were mainstays of commercial aviation for 20 years, before turbo props and jets finally displaced them. *Courtesy of the National Archives*

CHAPTER THREE

A little-known fact about Eisenhower is that he was a pilot himself, indeed the first president licensed to pilot an airplane, having soloed a Stearman PT-13 biplane trainer in the Philippines in 1936. Eisenhower was issued a private pilot's license on July 5, 1939, by the Commonwealth of the Philippines. He also had a Certificate of Competency from the U.S. Civil Aeronautics Authority. Eisenhower logged 350 hours of flying time from July 1936 to November 1939. Aboard his new presidential aircraft, however, Eisenhower was strictly a passenger.

By the time *Columbine II* was tapped for presidential duty, the aircraft had already carried President-Elect Eisenhower on his famous Far East trip of November 1952, fulfilling his campaign pledge to visit the war in Korea.

COLUMBINE II

Ike's C-121A was essentially a Lockheed Model 749 airliner with strengthened floors and a port rear fuselage cargo door. A graceful and elegant aircraft with its shark-like fuselage and triple tail,

Lockheed VC-121A Constellation 48-610 landing at New York's Idlewild Airport in November 1960. The plane had been President Eisenhower's personal transport, *Columbine II*, until being replaced by a later model Constellation in 1954. It continued to operate with the Air Force and was eventually sold to a civilian user. *Jim Hawkins*

A rare view of President Eisenhower's *Columbine II*. The official caption says that this color photo was taken at Washington National Airport in 1954. *USAF via Jim Kippen*

The Constellation's galley exudes a futuristic look, with clean, stainless steel surfaces. Note the aerodynamic, art deco look to the intercom handset. To serve the president, the Constellation's cabin was modified with leather swivel chairs, a table, couches that opened into beds, and a large lavatory. *Courtesy of the National Archives*

Columbine II was powered by four 2,500-horse-power Wright R-3350 (749C-18BD1) Cyclone piston engines.

To become a flying White House for the new president, the Constellation was removed from service and modified with the installation of a customized suite amidships. The 20-foot-long interior cabin was equipped with two brown leather swiveling chairs, a table, and two davenport couches, which opened into beds. A large lavatory was installed in the tail section. Forward of the presidential cabin were two duplicate cabins, each providing seating for 16 or sleeping berths for eight.

Because of its very important passenger, *Columbine II* became a VC-121A, the 'V' prefix signifying its role carrying dignitaries. The aircraft was equipped with the latest in flying instrumentation, including weather radar and Long Range Navigation (LORAN) equipment. A crew of eleven operated the VC-121A.

It should be noted that almost every aircraft operated by the Air Force to support the president wore the 'V' prefix at one time or another. The prefix has been added or removed under different administrations.

Quite remarkably, *Columbine II* is still flying today, the only presidential aircraft to have ended up in the hands of a civilian owner. A presidential seal from the aircraft, bearing 49 stars (as the seal did before Hawaii was admitted as a state), is on display at the Army's Quartermaster Museum at Fort Lee, Virginia.

COLUMBINE III

In 1954, Air Force leaders decided it was time for President Dwight D. Eisenhower to have a new aircraft for his personal transportation. Ike's C-121A Constellation, the *Columbine II*, was racking up a high number of flight hours (it had accumulated 4,000 before becoming the president's mount) and no longer represented up-to-date technology. With considerable input from pilot Draper, officials decided on a Lockheed 1049C Super Constellation, a longer, heavier aircraft with greater fuel capacity and more interior space.

The new aircraft was known in military jargon as a VC-121E Super Constellation (serial number 53-7885, constructor's number 4151) and was given the inevitable name *Columbine III*. It had been originally procured by the Navy as an R7V-1 model, bureau no. 131650, but was transferred to the Air Force before leaving the Burbank, California, factory.

The Air Force accepted Ike's VC-121E at the factory on August 31, 1954. Draper brought the aircraft to Washington National Airport on September 10. First Lady Mamie Eisenhower conducted a christening ceremony on November 24 using a bottle of Rocky Mountain spring water flown in from her beloved Colorado. That day, President Eisenhower made his first trip in the new aircraft, flying to Augusta, Georgia.

Columbine III ultimately spent six years as a

presidential aircraft. Unlike today's Air Force One, it was not used exclusively by the president, however. When Ike wasn't traveling, the VC-121E carried other government officials. This was probably a good deal for the taxpayers. After all, Ike only flew about 30,000 miles per year, a figure which today would rank him in the lowest category of an airliner's frequent flyer club.

Ike's VC-121E was powered by four Wright R-3350-34 (civilian model 972TV18DA-1) Turbo Compound engines. The new presidential transport was 18 feet longer than its predecessor, offered a range of 3,500 miles, and was able to fly at a speed of 355 miles per hour. Long after Eisenhower became the first president to have a jet aircraft assigned to him, the VC-121E continued to fly transport missions with the Air Force. Late in its career, it was redesignated C-121G.

First Lady Mamie Eisenhower christens the *Columbine III* with the traditional smashing of a bottle, on November 24, 1954. The photo provides a clear look at the Colorado state flower, from which the *Columbine* aircraft got their name. *Courtesy of the National Archives*

Beside the presidential seal, President and First Lady Eisenhower wave for the cameras. Before air travel became so commonplace, shots of the president arriving and departing on aircraft were fixtures of TV and print media. The president still typically waves when greeted at an airfield, but the image has become less common. *Courtesy of the National Archives*

INTRODUCING THE BOEING 707

During the Eisenhower administration, the jet engine became the primary source of power for new military, civil, and commercial aircraft, replacing propellers. A vigorous U.S. aircraft industry recognized a potential to make billions of dollars by converting the world's airlines from props to jets. A lucrative sidelight would be converting the Air Force's fleet of air-refueling tankers from propeller-driven to jet-powered aircraft.

In an era when corporations took more risks than today, Boeing gambled $16 million on the revolution it saw coming. On July 15, 1954, a yellow and maroon four-jet prototype aircraft took to the skies over Seattle. It was dubbed the Boeing

Long after serving as President Eisenhower's *Columbine III*, this Lockheed VC-121E Super Constellation (53-7885) continued to serve as an executive transport with the Air Force. At some point after losing its presidential portfolio, the aircraft was redesignated C-121G. Here, it is seen on a visit to Royal Air Force Mildenhall, England, in September 1967. *Brian Stainer*

Today, Americans are accustomed to seeing President George W. Bush travel on a giant aircraft, familiar to all as Air Force One. But in the 1950s, some Air Force members flew the president in a much smaller plane. For short trips from Washington to his beloved farm in Gettysburg, Pennsylvania, which had a grass runway, Dwight D. Eisenhower favored the Air Force's twin-engined Aero L-26B Commander.

In 1955, the Air Force issued a contract to Aero Design and Engineering Company of Bethany, Oklahoma, for a military version of the Aero Commander business aircraft. The L-26B (its "L" designation signifying a liaison function) became the first presidential aircraft to carry the now-familiar blue and white paint scheme. In the 1950s, the color scheme was known as Baltic blue and Polar white.

On June 3, 1955, the first flight of a president in a light plane took place when Ike made the 32-minute trip to Gettysburg in an Aero Commander Model 560 loaned to the White House by the manufacturer while the Air Force L-26Bs were still being built.

The Air Force eventually ordered 15 L-26B airplanes, all based on the improved Aero Commander Model 560A. They were each powered by two GO-480-G1B6 Lycoming piston engines providing 295 horsepower. The L-26B carried a crew of just two pilots, plus four to eight passengers at a cruising speed of 250 miles per hour.

The planes were stationed at Bolling Air Force Base in Washington, D.C. The presidential unit was the 1299th Air Transport Squadron of the 1254th Air Transport Wing, a predecessor of today's 99th Airlift Squadron, 89th Airlift Wing, at Andrews Air Force Base, Maryland.

Ike used one of these planes for frequent trips to Gettysburg. Fitted temporarily with a bed, the planes shuttled him back and forth during his recovery from a heart attack in the summer of 1955. He later flew in an L-26B to a March 26, 1956, meeting with American and international dignitaries at White Sulphur Springs, West Virginia.

The last two of the 15 aircraft in the Air Force's purchase were modified on the production line to Aero Commander 680 status. These two planes had improved Lycoming GSO-480-A1A6 engines providing 340 horsepower each, carried additional fuel, and were about 20 miles per hour faster.

The improved Commanders were called L-26Cs. Eisenhower made his first flight in an L-26C on June 6, 1956. One of these aircraft carried West German Chancellor Conrad Adenauer from New York City to Gettysburg. Eisenhower and Adenauer than traveled together in the aircraft to Washington.

The Air Force's Aero Commanders lost their presidential duties when Ike left office on January 20, 1961. By then, the radio call sign Air Force One had been adopted to refer to any Air Force plane carrying the chief executive. Also by that time, helicopters were able to take over short-range flights of the kind for which the L-26B and L-26C had been purchased.

The L-26B and L-26C fleet performed many other missions, in addition to flying the commander-in-chief. They were considered extremely reliable for general utility missions, and could land at small airfields where larger transports could not gain access.

In a change of military nomenclature that took place in 1962, the L-26B became the U-4A (for utility) and the L-26C became the U-4B. At least one U-4B was used in the 1960s by the Air Force Academy for cadet parachute training and for the Academy's skydiving team.

The L-26B or U-4B used by Eisenhower is now on display at the Air Force Museum in Dayton, Ohio.

367-80, taking its model number from the Stratocruiser series of prop-driven transports. To those who worked on it and flew it, the aircraft was called simply the "Dash 80." Until the plane was made public, its misleading name veiled the corporate secret that the aircraft was no Stratocruiser and had no props.

It helped Boeing that General Curtis E. LeMay of the Strategic Air Command wanted the new aircraft as an air-refueling tanker. The United States was fielding jet bombers capable of cruising speeds as high as 500 miles per hour, including the B-47 Stratojet, B-52 Stratofortress, and B-58 Hustler. They needed a gas station in the sky that could keep up.

On August 5, 1954, just three weeks after the maiden flight of the Dash 80, the USAF announced that it would purchase a limited number of jet tankers. The service eventually recruited 820 Boeing KC-135 Stratotankers, based on the Dash 80 and known in manufacturer's jargon as Boeing 717s. Test pilots "Dix" Loesch and "Tex" Johnston took the first KC-135A aloft for its maiden flight on August 31, 1956.

The first KC-135A became operational on June 28, 1957. By then, the race was on to field jet airliners, and the Air Force was seriously looking to the jet as a possible replacement for Eisenhower's *Columbine III*. By then, the Dash 80 test ship was equipped as a civil demonstrator for the airlines. Having given birth to a tanker, it would now spawn an airliner.

The first production Boeing 707 (constructor's number 17586) took to the air at Renton, Washington, on December 20, 1957. This plane wore civil registry numbering it as N708PA, making it appear to be the second of an initial batch of 20 707s for Pan American World Airways. The second aircraft in the series had been chosen for the special registration N707PA. As late as the second half of the 1950s, some skeptics were saying that these jetliners would never make the grade. In Britain, the Bristol company was still trying to convince the world that its

Britannia airliner—pulled through the sky by propellers—was the wave of the future. Bristol engineers asserted that the Boeing 707 design was too revolutionary to be harnessed for practical work, that the airframe and wing would require six engines rather than four, and that Boeing's aircraft was a monster, impossibly big, heavy, capacious, and expensive, needing long runways and ready to bankrupt airlines. Boeing had risked more than the company's net worth to build the prototype 367-80, was heavily in hock for the earliest 707s, and seemed to be taking a desperate gamble—but the airlines liked what Boeing was offering and were ready to leap into the future.

In an era when fewer than 10 percent of Americans had even seen the interior of any aircraft, airline travel was still the province of the privileged, and it took place in a realm where the future was now. Promoting glamour and sophistication, the airlines went for the graceful and futuristic Boeing 707 without hesitation and, surprisingly, with relatively few teething troubles.

The 707 made its first airline revenue flight on October 26, 1958, a scheduled service from New York to Paris. The Douglas DC-8 followed suit on September 18, 1959, and the Convair 880 on May 14, 1960.

Thinking much farther ahead than Bristol or anyone else who advocated propellers, the Air Force picked the Boeing 707 for presidential duty. In military parlance, the aircraft would be called the C-137A or VC-137A, dropping and regaining the "V" prefix several times in its career.

April 7, 1959, marked the first flight of the first military Boeing 707-153, a VC-137A model (58-6970, later to be named *Queenie*). Soon afterward, Boeing delivered *Queenie* to the 89th Wing at Andrews Air Force Base, Maryland. This aircraft was not earmarked for presidential travel but would become the first jet to carry a president.

Unlike the 707 airliner, the military VC-137A introduced a special communications section located in the forward fuselage, ahead of an eight-seat

In August of 1959, President Eisenhower departed for talks with Germany, England, and France, prior to the U.S. visit of Soviet Premier Nikita Khrushchev the following month. *Courtesy of the National Archives*

passenger compartment. The center cabin was configured as an airborne headquarters with conference table, swivel chairs, film projector, and divans convertible to beds. The aft compartment contained 14 reclining passenger seats. In all, the VC-137A would have been able to carry 40 passengers on a typical VIP trip.

On August 26, 1959, Eisenhower became the first president to fly aboard a jet, on *Queenie*, which was eventually used by seven presidents even though it was always considered only a backup. He flew to Germany for a meeting with Chancellor Konrad Adenauer. At this juncture, *Queenie* was attired in her initial paint scheme, which included

fluorescent red trim on nose, wingtips, and tail, a precaution taken as a result of the mid-air, broad-daylight collision of a United Airlines Douglas DC-7 and a Trans World Airlines Lockheed Constellation over the Grand Canyon in June 1956.

Andrews' elite air wing took delivery of three VC-137As in this series (serial numbers 58-6970–6972, constructor's numbers 17925–17927), the first of which was *Queenie*, but none of which was purchased with the intent of transporting the president. But only the first ship served repeatedly and frequently as a backup to presidential aircraft. Possibly without Eisenhower's knowledge, the Central Intelligence Agency outfitted *Queenie* with secret reconnaissance cameras in preparation for Ike's planned 1960 summit meeting in Moscow. That meeting was scuttled, ironically, because of the shooting down of Francis Gary Powers in his U-2 spy plane over the USSR on May 1, 1960.

Almost forgotten, however, is the fact that Eisenhower did travel to France for the proposed summit—by jet, meaning via *Queenie*. He was in Paris from May 15 to May 19, 1960. The term Air Force One had been in use for several years by that date. In 1962, *Queenie* carried astronaut John Glenn to Washington the day after his orbital flight.

Known initially as the VC-137A, this aircraft was powered by early, 13,500-pound-thrust Pratt & Whitney JT3C turbojet engines, with water injection and distinctive engine pods having multipipe nozzles. The large, noise-suppression nozzle with 20 separate tubes routinely became covered with soot from wet takeoffs, when black smoke was emitted in impressive amounts. Not long after their delivery, the Air Force retrofitted its trio of VC-137As with 18,000-pound-thrust Pratt & Whitney JT3D-3 turbofan engines and redesignated them as VC-137Bs.

A NEW CALL SIGN

During the mid-1950s the president's aircraft received a new radio call sign. There is disagreement, however, as to exactly when and how it happened—even among those who served as crew members on presidential aircraft. One former radio operator aboard *Columbine II* reports that the name Air Force One was created in a group conference at Washington National Airport. Others, however, insist that confusion during a flight was responsible for the new term, and that Ike's pilot, Draper, suggested it.

As the story goes, "Air Force 610" (the designation for *Columbine II*) was on a flight to Florida and was receiving radio instructions when "Eastern 610" (a commercial flight by Eastern Airlines) came on the airwaves. Whatever confusion took place was brief. No mishap occurred. But Draper

and others saw the event as a wake-up call. The president already enjoyed top priority when traveling the nation's airways (a "priority 1" according to some), but to prevent accidents, the chief executive needed to be quickly and readily identified.

The term "Air Force One" was born.

From about 1956 onward, any Air Force aircraft carrying the president became Air Force One. The aircraft of other services transporting the chief executive used call signs accordingly—Army One, Marine One. It is unclear whether a president has ever flown aboard a Navy aircraft. The Coast Guard, always a little different, continues to use the call sign Coast Guard One for its own boss, the Secretary of Transportation. Should the president fly on a civilian aircraft, it would use the call sign Executive One.

Today, everyone recognizes the term Air Force One. The term has become the title of a blockbuster movie starring Harrison Ford, a television special by *National Geographic* magazine, and a documentary by the Discovery Channel. It is familiar to air traffic controllers from Moscow to Monrovia. To many, Air Force One is a symbol of American sovereignty and influence.

RUDE AWAKENING

Once the new call sign for the president's aircraft had been coined, it was not widely announced or publicized. Even in the Air Force, many did not know about it right away. An anecdote clarifies how one officer learned.

In May 1960, Air Force Captain John W. Darr was serving with the 99th Bombardment Wing, a B-52 Stratofortress unit at Westover Air Force Base, Massachusetts. He recalls:

"I was one of two men who ran what we called the Current Operations Section. Because we were one of the very early B-52 outfits (the third, in fact), we were frequently tasked with performing 'higher headquarters directed' missions. I was also the point of contact within the wing for all matters related to coordination with federal aviation authorities.

Piasecki H-21B Workhorse 52-8684 touches down on the Ellipse in Washington, D.C., across the street from the south lawn of the White House. Helicopter crews practiced evacuation from the Executive Mansion—including bringing people out of a secret tunnel—but never actually carried the president. A different version of this image appeared on the cover of a Sunday newspaper supplement magazine in 1957. *Frank C. Fox*

"When we'd have a special mission planned, I'd coordinate the plan with Boston Center, who in turn would pass it on to CARF—Central Altitude Reservation Facility (or Function), which was located in Kansas City.

"Every such mission was assigned a priority. As I recall, priority 2 was for high-ranking individuals, 3 was an emergency in progress or in-flight refueling, 4 was for missions of some importance, while 5 was for routine military activity. I don't recall that I was aware of a priority 1.

"When flying on a priority 4 or 5, it was common for me to receive a phone call—often in the middle of the night, no less—from some guy at CARF. Over the phone we'd resolve conflicts, and life would proceed.

"One day, our outfit was in the midst of keeping two B-52s airborne around the clock on airborne alert. Because they were carrying nuclear weapons, we were operating on a priority 2. As a logical consequence, those midnight phone calls did not occur. If there were conflicts between our aircraft and others, I'm sure the other fellows were ordered to change their plans—but certainly not anyone with our top priority!

"You can imagine my surprise when I was awakened at about 3 o'clock one morning by a call from CARF. The fellow on the other end of the line told me that I would have to alter the route, altitude, or timing of our two-ship B-52 cell somewhere out over the Atlantic, east of Boston. In my mind I was trying to determine what best to do when I finally realized that my priority 2 was being challenged. I asked him, 'Who's asking us to move?' I asked.

"He responded with, 'Air Force One.' I had never heard the term before. (Later, I found that no

one else in my outfit had ever heard the term, either.) So I responded with, 'Who is that?'

He retorted with, 'My God, man—that's the PRESIDENT!'

"So I gave him a 'Really! OK, we'll move.' And I agreed to have our aircraft fly high enough to avoid the perceived conflict.

"The presidential mission that our B-52s had almost interfered with was the one carrying President Eisenhower to Paris for the Big Four summit, which the Soviet Union's Nikita Khrushchev refused to attend. My recollection is that Eisenhower was traveling in a Boeing 707 [a.k.a. *Queenie*]."

MARINE HELICOPTERS

On September 7, 1957, Eisenhower was vacationing in Newport, Rhode Island, when his presence was required immediately at the White House.

Typically, a return to Washington from Rhode Island called for an hour-long ferry ride across Narragansett Bay to the awaiting presidential airplane (then the *Columbine III*), followed by a 45-minute flight to Andrews and a 20-minute motorcade ride to the White House.

Ike directed his aide to find a way to get him to his airplane more quickly. The aide informed the president that a helicopter was on station in Rhode Island in case of emergency and could fly the president to the waiting plane. Eisenhower approved the idea and set a precedent with the seven-minute flight in a helicopter belonging to Marine Corps squadron HMX-1, later to be nicknamed the "Nighthawks." The helicopter used was apparently a Sikorsky HUS-1 Seahorse.

Shortly thereafter, the president's naval aide asked HMX-1 to evaluate landing a helicopter on the south lawn of the White House. The Marines chose the Sikorsky HSS-1Z, which was virtually identical to the HUS-1 (both were redesignated VH-34D when the system for naming military aircraft was altered in 1962). Preliminary evaluation and test flights determined that there was ample room for safe landing and departure. Indeed, soon afterward, the Air Force performed similar landings with the Piasecki H-21B Workhorse and Bell H-13J.

By 1959, Eisenhower was being routinely transported between the White House and Andrews by Marine helicopters as well as helicopters belonging to the Army. The Air Force continued to provide helicopters for possible emergency evacuation.

Beginning during the Eisenhower era, a number of aircraft were assigned to evacuate the president and other dignitaries in case of nuclear war or national emergency. One of the first was this H-19B helicopter (53-4436). The evacuation helicopters, which never actually carried a president, were assigned first to Olmstead Air Force Base near Harrisburg, Pennsylvania, and later to Andrews Air Force Base, where they eventually became part of the 89th Airlift Wing. *Frank C. Fox*

President Dwight D. Eisenhower emerging from Army One, a Sikorsky VH-34C, in 1958. *Pima Air and Space Museum*

For 18 years, between 1958 and 1976, the Army shared in the job of providing air transport for the President of the United States.

The Army's role is often forgotten today, as the public watches President George W. Bush travel in an Air Force airplane, familiar to Americans as Air Force One, or a Marine Corps helicopter, known in jargon as Marine One. But soldiers had a role in providing helicopter travel to five presidents, using a helicopter that became "Army One" when the president was on board.

In 1957, President Dwight D. Eisenhower began asking about the use of rotary-winged aviation as a means of presidential transportation. That year, Ike became the first commander-in-chief to fly aboard a helicopter when he took an Air Force Bell H-13J from the White House lawn to his retreat at Camp David, Maryland.

But although two H-13Js (known after 1962 as UH-13Js) were procured for presidential travel, the Secret Service questioned the margin of safety offered by a single-pilot craft. Ike flew in the H-13J only once, and the Air Force never again operated a helicopter dedicated to the presidential transport mission.

Also in 1957, Marine Corps squadron HMX-1, already in existence for a decade as a test unit, became the helicopter squadron for the personal transportation needs of the president. But Army leaders bristled. Ike was one of the most famous of Army generals, after all, and Army helicopter officers felt they could do the job as well as the Marines.

On January 1, 1958, the service activated the Army Executive Flight Detachment, at Davison Army Air Field, Fort Belvoir, Virginia. This squadron-sized unit, together with Marine squadron HMX-1 at Quantico, Virginia, were to share the primary mission of the emergency evacuation of the president, his family, and other key government officials. In addition to this mission, these units furnished helicopter transportation for the president and others.

The Army's aircraft of choice was the Sikorsky VH-34C Choctaw helicopter. This aircraft was almost identical to the HSS-1Z being used by the Marine unit (which was re-designated VH-34D in 1962).

The H-34 was powered by a 1,525-horsepower Wright R-1820-84 radial engine, was flown by two pilots, and could travel at up to 120 miles per hour with a range of 210 miles, making it ideal for Ike's jaunts to Camp David and his farm in Gettysburg, Pennsylvania.

In a memo dated 1960, VH-34C pilot Lieutenant Colonel William A. Howell noted that the VH-34C was "thoroughly reliable" for travel by the chief executive. The Secret Service agreed. On occasion, Ike and his successor President John F. Kennedy were offered a choice. The president would arrive at Andrews Air Force Base, Mary-land, step off his airplane, and find both Army and Marine H-34s waiting for him.

The term Army One as a radio call sign for any Army air-craft carrying the president came into use in 1960. Presidents Eisenhower, Kennedy, Johnson, Nixon, and Ford all flew in Army helicopters. To iron out their differences in an early example of "jointness," the two services with rotary wing aircraft combined their administrative functions in an Army–Marine Corps Executive Flight Detachment—but competition remained a part of everyday life.

The VH-34Cs piloted by Howell and other Army avia-tors with presidents as their cargo can still be viewed at museums. One is on display at the Army Aviation Museum, Fort Rucker, Alabama, another at the Pima Air and Space Museum in Tucson, Arizona.

The Army VH-34Cs were eventually replaced by VH-1 Iroquois (Huey) and VH-3 helicopters during the Nixon years.

In 1976, in a cost-cutting measure prompted by Pres-ident Jimmy Carter, the Pentagon decided to turn over the presidential helicopter mission to the Marines, and it has been carried out by HMX-1 ever since. The Army still pro-vides support but no longer operates helicopters earmarked for the president.

Both the Army and Marine Corps used the Sikorsky H-34 helicopter to carry presi-dents, although the Marines identified their version by other names prior to October 1, 1962, when all services adopted the same terminology for their aircraft. The 1957 Rhode Island helicopter trip by President Eisenhower apparently was made aboard a Marine HUS-1, as shown here. The Marines' HSS-1Z and HUS-1 were later redesignated VH-34D. *US Marine Corps*

On May 31, 1957, the first of two H-13J helicopters (57-2728) was put through its stuff on the White House lawn, flown by Major Joe Barrett. Barrett's recollection is is that President Eisenhower did not fly in the helicopter that day, not even for a brief demonstration, and that the president subsequently flew in the H-13J only once or twice. *Bell Helicopters/US Air Force*

President Dwight D. Eisenhower poses in a somewhat cramped H-13J (Model 47J-A-2) helicopter. Ike's smile is undoubtedly genuine, but the Secret Service was not exactly cheerful about entrusting the commander-in-chief to a single-engine, single-pilot helicopter, even though the H-13J had passed hundreds of hours or reliability tests. *Bell Helicopter*

A NEW PRESIDENT

During Senator John F. Kennedy's 1960 presidential campaign, his primary mode of transportation was a Convair 240 named *Caroline*, after his daughter. His father purchased the aircraft for him. In November 1960, Kennedy won a narrow election to the presidency and, soon afterward, visited Eisenhower in the White House. According to one observer, Eisenhower believed Kennedy was "a bit of a political lightweight." So during their first meeting at the White House, Eisenhower picked up the phone and called for a "Marine Condition Green." Three minutes later, a helicopter landed on the lawn ready to evacuate the president. Eisenhower made this demonstration in order to show Kennedy the power of the presidency.

The 1254th Air Transport Group was enlarged and redesignated the 1254th Air Transport Wing on December 1, 1960. The presidential wing was preparing to receive the first jet aircraft explicitly designed for presidential travel. This aircraft was the first of two special 707-353Bs ordered in 1961, designated VC-137C and assigned serial number 62-6000 (constructor's number 18461).

By then, the air crews who transported the president were referring to themselves as the SAM Fox outfit. SAM was the abbreviation for Special Air Mission, and Fox was the old phonetic term for the letter "F," as in flight, so the term was an acronym for "Special Air Mission Flight." The new presidential plane was Air Force One to the outside world, but to insiders it was SAM 26000.

SAM 26000 arrived at Andrews on October 10, 1962. When the spanking new jet entered service, it was capable of traveling farther and faster than any other executive aircraft in the Air Force fleet. It could also operate from much shorter runways.

To all who maintained it, worked on it, and flew it, SAM 26000 was the most beautiful plane they had ever seen. It represented a new age, just

Although President Kennedy's favorite aircraft was the prop-driven C-118A, for short trips Army and Marine helicopters were available. Here, the president debarks from a Sikorsky H-3 on the White House lawn. *Photo courtesy John F. Kennedy Library*

President John F. Kennedy walks in front of a Lockheed VC-140B JetStar (61-2491), the small, four-jet executive aircraft in which he flew occasionally on short trips. The JetStar later was used to carry Lyndon B. Johnson to his Texas ranch. At the center of this blurred image, apparently taken in early 1963, is the 565-gallon slipper fuel tank mounted at approximately mid-point between root and tip on the JetStar's 30-degree swept wing. *Pima Air and Space Museum*

President Kennedy used the versatile Sikorsky H-3 helicopter for short trips, such as this one to the U.S. Naval Academy in Annapolis, Maryland. As the chief executive steps onto the Dewey athletic field, a sailor draws his hand back to salute. *Courtesy of the National Archives*

like the new and youthful president who seemed not to be living the past but pointing to the future.

Encouraged by the president, First Lady Jacqueline Kennedy commissioned the noted designer Raymond Loewy to devise a new paint scheme for the White House's new jet. Loewy was, of course, designer of the Studebaker Avanti automobile, the Pennsylvania Railroad paint scheme, and the Ritz cracker logo. He also created the designs for the Coca Cola bottle, the Lucky Strike cigarette package, and Greyhound Buses.

Until now, the upper fuselage of an Air Force transport had borne the words "United States Air Force" or "Military Air Transport Service." Both were standard examples of military markings, but the Kennedys wanted to show that SAM 26000 represented more than just a part of the Air Force and, indeed, more than the entire Air Force.

Loewy may have been inspired by the blue and white paint design that had adorned Eisenhower's twin-engined L-26B Aero Commander. He cast aside standard military markings. Instead, SAM 26000 would bear the words "United States of America," making it an aerial ambassador, of sorts. The presidential VC-137C wore an American flag on the tail (with the union, the blue field containing

SAM 26000, a Boeing VC-137C aircraft, served presidents, senior representatives, and heads of state. At President Kennedy's request, industrial designer Raymond Loewy helped design the plane's distinctive appearance. The blue and white color scheme has carried through more or less to the present day. The first jet designed for presidential use, the VC-137C could travel farther and faster than any other executive aircraft in the fleet, and could operate from much shorter runways than its predecessors. *Courtesy of the National Archives*

SAM 26000 was delivered to the 1254th Air Transport Group (which evolved into the 89th Airlift Wing) on July 10, 1961. VC-137C Stratoliner 62-6000 was piloted by Colonel James B. Swindall when it carried Presidents Kennedy and Johnson. Colonel Ralph Albertazzi was the presidential pilot when SAM 26000 carried President Nixon. *USAF via Jim Kippen*

Interior view of the Boeing VC-137 aircraft, at Andrews Air Force Base in Maryland. VC-137 was the military designation of the plane built for the commercial market as a Boeing 707. *Courtesy of the National Archives*

A close-up of the wing and tail sections of the SAM 26000, VC-137C. The American flag appeared on both sides of the fin, with the blue field of stars facing fore on both sides. Designer Raymond Loewy actually toned down the blue on the flag so that it would better match the rest of the aircraft's color scheme. The VC-137C had a wingspan of 145 feet 9 inches. *Courtesy of the National Archives*

During the Cuban missile crisis of October 1962, the naval air station at Boca Chica, Key West, Florida, was the staging point for U.S. aerial reconnaissance missions over Cuba. Because of the base's outstanding efforts during that period, President John F. Kennedy visited the base shortly after Thanksgiving 1962 to provide his thanks in person. *Photo courtesy John F. Kennedy Library*

50 stars, facing forward on both sides of the fin, as correct usage dictated), a striking blue and white paint job, and large replicas of the presidential seal on both sides of the nose. To make the colors match as planned, Loewy even toned down the blue in the national insignia on the rear fuselage.

Except for the presidential seal, a similar paint scheme was eventually adopted by all of the VIP aircraft at Andrews.

Two days after arriving at Andrews, the aircraft made its first official flight, to Wheelus Air Base, Libya, to bring that country's crown prince to the United States for a visit. As the Cuban missile crisis loomed immediately after it entered service, SAM 26000 brought senators and congressmen from their home states to Washington, since Congress was not in session at the time. President Kennedy

The last presidential propliner, a Douglas C-118A Liftmaster (52-3240) of the 89th Airlift Wing, landing at Kennedy International Airport, New York, in September 1964. A favorite of John F. Kennedy, this military version of the DC-6 airliner endured well into the jet age. *Jim Hawkins*

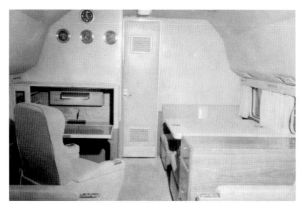

This interior shot of President Kennedy's Douglas C-118 reveals the cabin's clock and instruments, desk with swivel chair, plus a booth and other seating to accommodate the president's family, guests, or advisers. The padding on the cabin walls likely helped make the cabin quieter. *Courtesy of the National Archives*

The presidential C-118A Liftmaster (52-3240) remained in service long after the jet-propelled VC-137C was introduced—and remained a favorite of President Kennedy for travels to Massachusetts. The caption for this official shot of the C-118A indicates it was taken in 1961 at Andrews. *USAF via Jim Kippen*

flew 26000 for the first time in November 1962, when he and the first lady attended Eleanor Roosevelt's funeral in New York. In June 1963, Kennedy used the aircraft when he flew to Ireland and Germany, where he made his famous "Ich Bin Ein Berliner" speech. A month earlier, while taking a U.S. delegation to Moscow, 26000 broke 30 speed records, including the fastest nonstop flight between the United States and the Soviet Union.

CARRYING KENNEDY

Kennedy frequently used SAM 26000 and its backup, *Queenie*. He also made regular use of the Army and Marine helicopters now available to the chief executive. But Kennedy's favorite aircraft was a prop-driven C-118A, the military version of the Douglas DC-6 and a close relative of the *Independence*, used by his predecessor once-removed, Harry S. Truman.

This C-118A (serial 53-3240) had been delivered to the 1254th Air Transport Wing at Washington National Airport on December 23, 1955. Always a VIP transport, it apparently never transported Eisenhower. In July 1961, it moved with the wing to Andrews. During this period, it carried Kennedy to his home in Hyannisport, Massachusetts, on numerous occasions. In the subsequent administration, it would be one of numerous aircraft to carry Lyndon B. Johnson to his Texas ranch. Air Force records refer to this aircraft both as a C-118A and a VC-118A. Of all the aircraft in the history of presidential travel, this one is the most ambiguous: Was it intended from the beginning as a presidential transport, or was it another "almost" presidential aircraft that did, in fact, carry presidents on more than a few occasions? The record is unclear.

As for SAM 26000, it flew John and Jacqueline Kennedy on their visit to Dallas on November 22, 1963. When news that the president had been shot reached Love Field and 26000's commander, Colonel James Swindall, the aircraft was prepared for immediate departure. Vice President Lyndon Johnson was also in Dallas that day. Fearing a wider conspiracy, Secret Service agents rushed now-President Johnson to the safety of the Air Force aircraft, Because the communications equipment of 26000 was superior to that of the aircraft that Johnson had flown to Dallas, the decision was made that Johnson should wait aboard 26000 for Jacqueline Kennedy and her husband's body. Crew members felt it would be undignified for the former president's body to ride back to Andrews in the cargo hold. However, making room for the casket in the

passenger compartment meant removing a partition and four seats from the rear of the aircraft. Before 26000 could leave Dallas, President Johnson took the oath of office on board the aircraft. At Arlington National Cemetery, as the president's body was being lowered into the ground, 26000 flew overhead at 1,000 feet and dipped its wings in final salute.

The body of President John F. Kennedy returns from Dallas, arriving at Andrews aboard VC-137C 62-6000. Jacqueline Kennedy, Robert F. Kennedy, and other figures are visible in this sequence of shots showing the Aerial Port unit using a catering van to lower the slain leader's casket from the aircraft to an ambulance. Today, the 89th Airlift Wing has flexible unloading devices called Ambu-Lifts, which would perform this function far more efficiently. *USAF*

CHAPTER 4

CAMELOT TO THE GIPPER

At the time of Kennedy's death, jetliners were securing their hold on the airways of the nation as well as the world. Jets were replacing props in the air-refueling community, and the Boeing 707 was the best-known aircraft in the world. Perhaps the ultimate 707 during this time was SAM 26000, which served as Air Force One. This, of course, was the aircraft aboard which Lyndon B. Johnson was sworn into office as the 36th president of the United States.

Although SAM 26000 (designated VC-137C) carried special communications equipment, its interior furnishings were little different from those of the three VC-137A/B (Boeing 707-153) aircraft also assigned to Andrews Air Force Base. SAM 26000 was continuously backed up by the ubiquitous VC-137A/B known as *Queenie*, which had a crew of two pilots, navigator, flight engineer, and two communications operators, but usually carried only one communicator. SAM 26000 had the same

SAM 26000, which carried presidents and other dignitaries for decades, returns to the United States from an overseas flight. The plane became Air Force One when the president was aboard. This VC-137C provided transportation for seven U.S. presidents during its long years of service. *Courtesy of the National Archives*

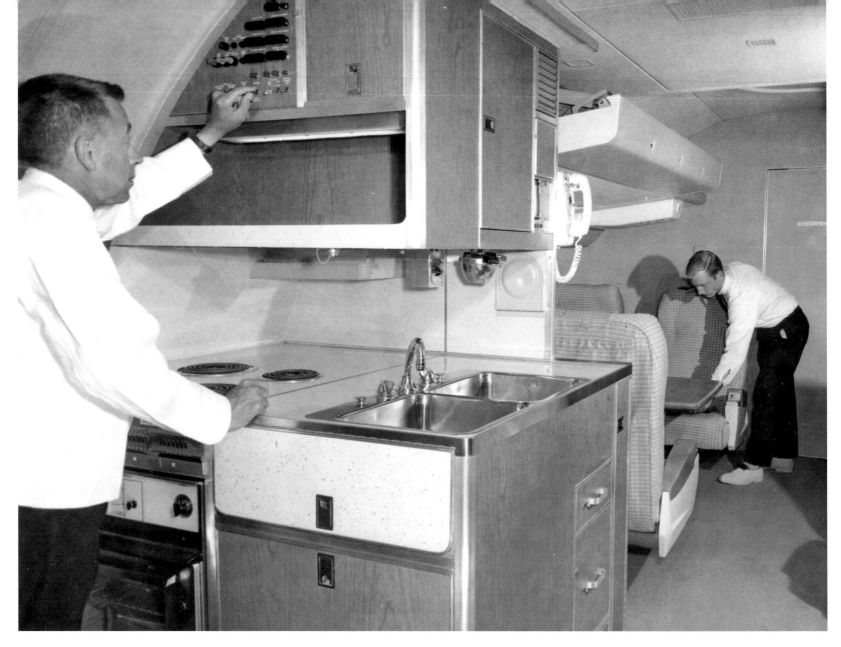

The VC-137C's galley photographed in 1965. Note the relatively open four-burner stove, bounded by walls on only two sides. Modern aircraft have more contained heating devices to reduce the risk of someone getting burned in the event the plane encounters turbulence. *Courtesy of the National Archives*

number of flight crew but always carried two communicators, plus four security forces personnel and four stewards.

Johnson, who liked to call SAM 26000 "my own little plane," used a variety of aircraft to travel to his Texas ranch. But whether it was a sleek Boeing 707 or a chugging, sputtering Convair, Johnson was a master at giving rides to those whose influence he needed. No other president was so adept at giving out the perk of a ride aboard Air Force One—or withholding it—but all presidents have used their magic carpet in the sky as a way of impressing and influencing other political leaders.

John Trimble, a radio operator on Air Force One during LBJ's tenure, recalls how the president enjoyed the perks of his flying White House:

"When talking on the radio, Johnson would lean back in his big chair, which had been specially installed and we had dubbed the throne, and talk with his subjects toiling far below. He could raise or lower the chair and desktop with the touch of a button. The [radio operator] was obliged to monitor these radio calls in order to take quick remedial action should it be necessary, as it frequently was. It was interesting listening, but I was always glad when the calls were over because I could catch up

Above: The main passenger compartment aboard the president's VC-137C aircraft contained 24 reclining seats, two typing desks and four pullman-style sleeping berths. *Courtesy of the National Archives*

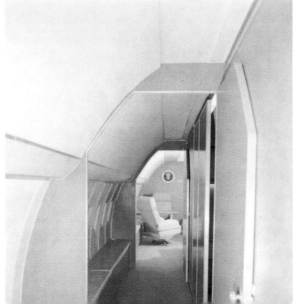

Left: This photo down a narrow hallway gives a good feel of what it would be like to move around on VC-137C. The presidential seal is aligned with the hallway, perhaps to remind those approaching president's cabin to do so quietly. *Courtesy of the National Archives*

A long-serving, "almost presidential" aircraft with the 89th Airlift
Wing was this Convair VC-131H
Samaritan (54-2816). Here, the
aircraft is seen on October 13,
1966, at Wilmington, Delaware,
during a visit by President Lyndon
Johnson to observe the return of
casualties from Vietnam at nearby
Dover Air Force Base. LBJ enjoyed
using the twin-engined Convair
for jaunts to his Texas ranch.
Richard S. Sullivan

Those who remember him say President Lyndon Johnson reveled in taking visitors to his Texas ranch aboard
the Convair VC-131H Samaritan, a twin-engined, turboprop aircraft known in civilian jargon as a Convair 580.
Looking down from his "king chair," a hydraulically-oper-
ated seat allowing Johnson—already a big man—to tower
above his companions, the president regaled them with
war stories and sometimes arm-twisted for a much-needed
vote on Capitol Hill. A pilot from the era remembers,
"Johnson was better than any other president at using a
ride in an airplane as a perk for congressmen he wanted to
impress. On those occasions when the VC-131H operated

as Air Force One, LBJ invited senators and congressmen to
travel with him and they became putty in his hands."

The 89th Military Airlift Wing operated four VC-131Hs.
The planes had originally been built as ordinary Air Force
transports under the designation C-131D, powered by two
2,500-horsepower Pratt & Whitney R-2800-103W Double
Wasp, twin-row, 18-cylinder reciprocating engines. The first
C-131D (54-2806) made its first flight on July 28, 1954.

The U.S. armed forces had used military versions of
the Convair 340 airliner since the first MC-131A Samaritan medical evacuation aircraft (52-5781), first flown on
March 5, 1954, and delivered on April 1, 1954. The first

U.S. Navy R4Y-1Z version (bureau no. 140378) was delivered to Naval Air Station Anacostia, Washington, D.C., in April 1955 for use by the Assistant Secretary of the Navy. More than a dozen versions of the C-131 served in all branches of the U.S. armed forces, which also operated T-29 (Convair 240) trainers and R4Y-2 (Convair 440) transports.

2,900-shp Allison T56-A-3 turboprop engines powered the sometimes-presidential VC-131Hs. On completing their 89th Wing duties, they were transferred to the District of Columbia Air National Guard. One of them (54-2816) suffered damage beyond repair when its landing gear accidentally retracted while on the ramp at Greenville, Texas, on May 12,

1977. The remaining three were transferred to a detachment of Naval Reserve squadron VR-52 in 1978. This unit was redesignated VR-48 in 1981. On November 15, 1985, three Navy crewmembers lost their lives when one of the aircraft (54-2817) crashed on takeoff at Dothan, Alabama.

The operational career of the Convair C-131 ended on August 30, 1990, when VR-48 transferred the last aircraft (55-0299) to the Department of State. In its new civilian guise, the C-131H was assigned to Peru to support Peruvian National Police in drug interdiction activity.

After they finished flying dignitaries, including on rare occasion the president, the Air Force's four Convair VC-131H Samaritans (including 54-2817, shown) were transferred to the Navy and continued duties at Andrews. This VC-131H portrait at Andrews was snapped in March 1983. *Joseph G. Handelman*

They called it SAM 26000. President Lyndon Johnson inherited this Boeing VC-137C Stratoliner (serial number 62-6000, constructor's number 18461) as his flying White House. This version of the Boeing 707-352B was destined to remain in service for decades. The aircraft underwent several changes in paint scheme, the one shown here coming late in its career. It also lost and regained its "V" prefix several times. This angle places emphasis on the podded TF33 turbofan engines, which extend about twelve feet forward of the leading edge of the swept-back wing. *Jim Kippen*

on some of my other duties. Johnson employed a mode of operation that he repeated over and over again. He would call a person to seek advice on a particular subject and infer that this person would be his only input prior to making an important decision. He would then talk with two or three different people on that subject using the same approach. I wonder if these 'wise counselors' ever talked among themselves."

Johnson reconfigured the interior of SAM 26000. Additional seats were added, and the seats were reversed to face the rear of the aircraft— toward the president's compartment. Johnson liked to be able to keep an eye on his passengers, and the cherry wood partitions that separated the passengers from the stateroom were replaced with clear plastic dividers. President Johnson used SAM 26000 and other aircraft extensively on travels back and forth between Washington and his Texas ranch. He was also a world traveler and used the aircraft for his flights to Vietnam at the height of the war.

Lyndon B. Johnson during a visit to Vietnam on Air Force One. The VC-137C flew the president to Cam Ranh Bay. *U.S. Air Force*

JOHNSON'S 118

For at least two months following the dark hours of the Kennedy assassination, Johnson refused to fly in Air Force One, for reasons unclear. At Andrews, rumors abounded, even the rumor that the president would begin flying via commercial airline.

President Johnson talks with Arthur J. Goldberg on Air Force One, shortly after appointing him U.S. Ambassador to the United Nations in July 1965. Goldberg replaced Adlai Stevenson, who died earlier that month in London. *Courtesy of the National Archives*

But Johnson never stopped using the VC-140 JetStars and VC-131H Samaritans that often took him to Texas—so often that one of each was periodically stationed on a semi-permanent basis at Bergstrom Air Force Base near Austin.

Moreover, Johnson frequently asked Washington luminaries to join him as he continued to fly aboard the VC-118A, military version of the Douglas DC-6 (53-3240), which his predecessor Kennedy had so thoroughly enjoyed. Johnson used a variety of aircraft to bring himself and visitors to his Texas ranch, but he also took the VC-118A else-

where. A two-day October 1964 trip took the president to Teterboro, New Jersey, for a speech, then to Wilkes-Barre, Pennsylvania, then to New York's La Guardia Airport. The trip continued to Rochester, then Buffalo, then New York, and finally back to Andrews. Johnson always made a point to be accompanied by as many people as possible, but on this trip, as on most, he was shadowed by his personal aide, Jack Valenti, a World War II B-25 Mitchell pilot later to be well known as the chief lobbyist for the motion picture industry. Valenti told the author of this volume that Johnson,

At a conference table aboard Air Force One, President Lyndon B. Johnson talks with aids on a flight from Washington to Honolulu in 1966. The subject is a meeting with South Vietnam chiefs, to which they were en route. *Courtesy of the National Archives*

The Air Force's sole Beech VC-6A (56-7943) was purchased expressly to meet Lyndon B. Johnson's needs and became "Lady Bird's airplane." It was one of several aircraft that spent considerable time at Bergstrom Air Force Base near Austin, Texas, servicing the Johnson ranch. Late in its career, the VC-6A doffed Air Force markings and national insignia and acquired the "plain Jane" color scheme shown here, making it difficult to distinguish from a civilian aircraft. *U.S. Air Force*

"Lady Bird's airplane" was the term used by President Johnson to identify the Beech VC-6A, military version of the King Air B90 with a special VIP interior (serial number 66-7943, constructor's number LJ-91). The Air Force acquired only one C-6, and it was never used for any purpose except to support the occupant of the White House.

Powered by two 550-horsepower Pratt & Whitney PT6A-20 turboprop engines and crewed by two pilots, the 109-passeger VC-6A had full pressurization for travel comfort at high altitude and all-weather navigation and de-icing equipment.

The Air Force shelled out $436,000 to purchase the C-6 for the very specific purpose of meeting Johnson's needs. During the early part of its operational career, it was used to transport Johnson and members of his family between Bergstrom Air Force Base, Texas, near Austin, and the Johnson family ranch near Johnson City. During this time, the aircraft became informally known as the "Lady Bird Special." After leaving presidential service, the VC-6A continued in its special executive transport role with the 89th Military Airlift Wing until it was retired to the USAF Museum—to which it was flown on September 6, 1985.

unlike Kennedy, had "no special attachment" to the VC-118A.

The VC-118A apparently ended its presidential duties in August 1967 when it was transferred to Europe. The aircraft was retired in June 1975 and is on display today at the Pima Air and Space Museum in Tucson, Arizona.

SAM 26000

As for the VC-137C, now better known to the public simply as Air Force One and to its users as SAM 26000, it was the ultimate version of the Boeing 707. It boasted a new, high-efficiency wing of 11 feet 7 inches greater span than earlier models, giving the wing a new span of 145 feet 9 inches. The fuselage was 8 feet 5 inches longer than earlier 707s, for a total of 152 feet 11 inches. The new gross weight was 312,000 pounds. With its blue and white exterior

and "United States of America" emblazoned on its fuselage, the aircraft seemed even more dazzling and glamorous than the 707s that were beginning to operate regularly on airline routes.

SAM 26000 set many point-to-point speed records flying from Andrews across the Atlantic. It was powered by the same 18,000-pound-thrust Pratt & Whitney JT3D-3 turbofan engines that were belatedly retrofitted on its non-presidential cousins, the VC-137B models. The engines enabled Air Force One to reach a speed of 625 miles per hour. The four-member flight crew of pilot, co-pilot, navigator, and flight engineer sat forward of an eight-seat VIP compartment with galley and toilets. In the center fuselage was an airborne headquarters with conference tables, swivel chairs, projection screen, and catnap bunks. The rear section had 14 double reclining chairs, tables, galleys, and toilets.

Although it was not originally designed as a presidential aircraft, the Lockheed VC-140 JetStar (61-2488, shown here) proved ideal for some of President Johnson's domestic travels, including trips to his Texas ranch. The JetStars were normally used for short- and medium-distance travel by other government officials, and did not usually carry the presidential seal seen here on the nose. *USAF via Jim Kippen*

An aircraft displayed in front of the passenger terminal at Andrews Air Force Base is a reminder of the era when the C-140 JetStar flew important missions for the Air Force. The JetStar was the first civilian business jet to be adopted for military use. The Air Force flew it from 1961 to 1989.

In the 1950s, the Air Force wanted jets to replace small, propeller-driven trainers and transports. One ideal candidate seemed to be the JetStar, designed by a Lockheed engineering team led by Kelly Johnson.

After looking at the JetStar on the drawing board, the Air Force selected it as a multi-engined trainer and ordered ten planes, to be called the T-40A. But in 1958, the service reversed this decision and ordered the more economical

T-39A Sabreliner. The Air Force cancelled the T-40A contract, and none was ever built.

Soon afterward, the Air Force acquired five C-140A Jet-Stars to be used to calibrate ground-based navigational aids in a mission known as "facilities checking." The first of these planes went to Scott Air Force Base, Illinois, in 1961. In later years, the planes operated at Clark Air Base, Philippines; Ramstein Air Force Base, Germany; and Richards-Gebaur Air Force Base, Missouri. The planes carried two pilots, a flight mechanic, and two enlisted technicians.

Subsequently, the service acquired five C-140B 13-seaters and six VC-140B JetStar eight-seat executive transports. The service quickly modified all 11 of these

planes to the VC-140B standard. These were assigned to Andrews Air Force Base, to provide transport to the nation's leaders. The planes carried two pilots and a steward. One VC-140B was used regularly in the 1960s to carry President Lyndon B. Johnson between Washington and his ranch in Texas. For a time, a VC-140B was stationed at Bergstrom Air Force Base near Austin, Texas, one of several aircraft (including a VC-131H Samaritan and Beech VC-6A) that became "Texans" during Johnson's tenure.

In later years, the facilities-checking C-140As were painted in camouflage and traveled as far as Vietnam to check navigational facilities. The facilities-checking mission remained in the Air Force until the 1990s, when it

was taken over by the Federal Aviation Administration.

All Air Force JetStars were powered by four 3,000-pound thrust Pratt & Whitney J60-P-5 turbojet engines, better known by their civilian term, JT12A-6. Typically, they had a cruising speed of 507 miles per hour.

Ironically, the airplane displayed at Andrews, although attired in military markings, isn't a military C-140 model at all. The display plane is a former civilian JetStar that never flew for the Air Force. A real VC-140B, one that was frequently used in the 1960s to transport Vice President Hubert Humphrey, is displayed at the Air Force Museum at Wright-Patterson Air Force Base, Ohio. Another can be seen at the Pima Air Museum, Tucson, Arizona.

The VC-140 is shown here at Andrews Air Force Base, Maryland, in 1966. *Courtesy of the National Archives*

With his characteristic "peace sign" gesture, President Richard Nixon exits Air Force One with First Lady Pat Nixon. This shot provides a close look at the blue trim on SAM 26000. When industrial designer Raymond Loewy helped style the look of the plane, he changed the shade of the blue field on the American flag on the plane's fin so that it would not contrast unfavorably with the plane's blue trim. *Courtesy of the National Archives*

As much as Johnson doted over SAM 26000, his successor seemed to take it for granted. When Richard Nixon became the 37th president on January 20, 1969, he began using the much-traveled Boeing 707 immediately. Nixon did not schmooze with the crew, however.

John Trimble, communications operator on the VC-137C, remembered, "LBJ was all over 'his' airplane. Nixon would give a wan little smile, greet the people within his immediate path, and disappear into his stateroom." Trimble recalls that presidential

pilot Ralph Albertazzi said that during the five and one-half years Albertazzi flew Nixon, the president never paid a visit to the flight deck.

WORLD TRAVELER

After the Johnson presidency, SAM 26000 continued its frequent travels. Nixon was in office less than a month when he made his first trip abroad SAM 26000, to Vietnam.

Shortly after Nixon's inauguration in January 1969, SAM 26000 went back to the Boeing factory

In 1971, President Nixon gave SAM 26000 the official name *The Spirit of '76*, in honor of the approaching American bicentennial. The name was transferred to the new presidential aircraft, SAM 27000, when it arrived in 1972, but most people continued to call that plane Air Force One. Nixon's family preferred the layout of the older plane and whenever they traveled together, they specified SAM 26000. *Courtesy of the National Archives*

for its first major overhaul. The aircraft was stripped to its metal shell from cockpit to tail. While engineers tested the aircraft's structure and systems, the interior layout was redesigned. The private quarters of the president were moved to the area forward of the wings, the most quiet and stable area of the aircraft. A staff compartment was built in the rear of SAM 26000.

Ironically, one feature of SAM 26000 that did not carry over into the Nixon administration was the taping system on board. By orders of the president,

This seating area, and the galley behind it, lie in the aft portion of *The Spirit of '76*. The headsets, which may appear to be part of a conferencing system, are not much different from those found on a commercial airliner. Their primary purpose is to allow passengers to listen to music. *Courtesy of the National Archives*

President Nixon's pilot was Colonel Ralph D. Albertazzie, seen here at the controls of VC-137 at Norton Air Force Base, California, in 1972. *Courtesy of the National Archives*

An Air Force One crew member types a radio message aboard VC-137 en route to Norton Air Force Base, California, in 1972. *Courtesy of the National Archives*

the system that recorded all incoming and outgoing calls on 26000 was removed.

In July 1969 President Nixon flew aboard SAM 26000 on a 13-day trip to six countries, culminating in a stop to meet the Apollo 11 crew in the middle of the Pacific Ocean.

In 1970, National Security Advisor Henry Kissinger used SAM 26000 to take him to the first of 13 secret meetings with officials from North Vietnam. Flying these secret missions was a major undertaking. They were even kept secret from the secretary of defense, secretary of state, and director of central intelligence. In 1971 Nixon gave 26000 an official name, *The Spirit of '76*, in honor of the coming bicentennial. A year later the name would be transferred to the newly-arrived second presidential aircraft, SAM 27000, but most continued to refer to it as Air Force One. In February 1972, SAM 26000 flew President Nixon on his historic visit to China, the first step in normalizing relations with the world's most populous country.

SAM 26000, dubbed *The Spirit of '76* by President Nixon, rests on the tarmac at Norton Air Force Base, California, in 1972. Note how the stars portion of the flag points fore, as custom requires. *Courtesy of the National Archives*

President Richard Nixon gazes from the window of *The Spirit of '76*. Perhaps to avoid any luggage mix-ups with passengers sharing his initials, his briefcase is labeled "The President." *Courtesy of the National Archives*

ENTER SAM 27000

The arrival of SAM 27000 was a milestone. Beginning in 1972, it was no longer necessary for the VC-137B named *Queenie* to back up Nixon's flying White House. Now, the second presidential Boeing 707 came on the scene, wearing serial number 72-7000 and known for short as SAM 27000. Unlike *Queenie*, the new VC-137C was meant from the start solely for presidential travel, and served in that role from the beginning.

In fact, SAM 27000 replaced SAM 26000 as the primary aircraft for presidential travel, making it, in effect, the new Air Force One. Despite this change, the Nixon family preferred the interior layout of the older plane, and traveled aboard her whenever the family flew together.

Although its physical dimensions restrict in many ways the degree of comfort the aircraft can provide, the place settings aboard *The Spirit of '76* are first class. This shot was taken at Norton Air Force Base in 1972. *Courtesy of the National Archives*

This shot shows some of the articles that President Nixon and his staff used aboard Air Force One up to 1972. *Courtesy of the National Archives*

CAMELOT *to the* GIPPER

With the blinds drawn, President Nixon meets aboard Air Force One with Vice President Gerald R. Ford, Secretary of State Henry Kissinger, former Attorney General John Mitchell and former Secretary of State William Rogers. *Courtesy of the National Archives*

SECURITY CONCERNS

The 1970s were a decade of hijackings and terror, and it was natural that experts would look for ways to protect Air Force One. Air Force officials are loath to say much about it, but open sources disclose that both VC-137Cs were equipped with an infrared countermeasures self-defense system (ISDS) to protect the aircraft against heat-seeking missiles.

Developed from an earlier system called the AN/ALQ-144, ISDS was a fuselage- or pylon-mounted item designed to provide protection from anti-aircraft missiles employing infrared homing devices. The system consisted of a multiband infrared countermeasures (IRCM) transmitter system, an electronic control unit, and operator control unit. The system configuration varied according to the type of aircraft, but for most installations it provided one transmitter per engine, with an associated electronic control unit. On the presidential VC-137Cs, the system was contained in rearward-facing fairings immediately above the rear of each of the planes' four engines.

Air Force officers will not say how the defensive unit is manned or controlled. But according to literature published on the system, a single-operator control unit located in the cockpit controls one to

SAM 27000 flying over Mt. Vernon, George Washington's home, in 1977. This plane, built in 1972, was a successor VC-137 to SAM 26000. Unlike its predecessor, SAM 27000 was intended exclusively for presidential travel. *Courtesy of the National Archives*

On Armed Forces Day, 1969, President Richard Nixon debarks a Sikorsky VH-3A Sea King helicopter during a visit to the aircraft carrier, USS *Saratoga. Courtesy of the National Archives*

This Piasecki H-21B-PH Workhorse (52-8701) of the 1001st Helicopter Flight, Military Air Transport Service (MATS), is flying near Andrews (and near the newly-constructed Washington Beltway, the famous thoroughfare encircling the capital) in about 1962. The H-21B fleet rehearsed landing on the south lawn of the White House to evacuate the president, but never actually had to execute a real-life rescue. *Frank C. Fox*

four transmitters. Weight of the transmitter is 65 pounds, and weight of the electronic control unit is 5 pounds. The operator control unit is a standard panel-mounted box measuring 146x125x57mm and weighing about 2 pounds.

The system would be useful on any military aircraft, of course—the vision of terrorists or military irregulars setting up shop near an airport and popping off with shoulder-mounted, heat-seeking missiles is a traveler's nightmare—but it's apparently expensive, and is employed in only about 150 turboprop and jet aircraft in production for U.S. and Allied air forces.

ARMY HELICOPTER

While SAM 26000 received improvements for its role as Air Force One, the Marine Corps and Army continued to share the mission of hauling the chief executive on short trips via helicopter. A Marine officer told the author of this volume that Nixon "pretty much took the helicopters for granted" and showed no special interest in aviation or in the configuration of the aircraft. "But he was always amicable toward us, even when he appeared lost in thought on deep issues."

By now, the Army helicopters were part of an Executive Flight Detachment, commanded during Nixon's term by Lieutenant Colonel Gene Boyer. He was also the pilot who flew Nixon from the White House to Andrews when the president resigned in August 1974. Co-pilot on that flight was CW4 Carl Burhanan. Nixon made his last flight from the White House lawn in Army One.

Although the crews and the cultures were separate, the Sikorsky VH-3A ("a blend of the civilian Sikorsky S-61 and the Navy SH-3A," according to a pilot) and Bell VH-1N Iroquois (Huey) helicopters operated by Marines and Army crews for the president were indistinguishable. All wore the same color scheme and the same words on the fuselage: "United States of America." Clint Downing, one of the Army helicopter pilots, told the author, "The only way you could distinguish which crew was flying was by their uniforms."

Downing adds, "During the time I was there we [the Army] shared the missions equally with the Marines. We alternated trips, that is on one trip we would go ahead and preposition at the destination and travel with the President. The Marines would pick him up on the lawn and take him to Andrews and then meet him upon his return. On the next trip this procedure would be reversed. The Marines would travel ahead and we would pick him up from the lawn and meet him on the return.

"Army and Marine VH-3s and the VH-1Ns were absolutely identical in every minute detail. Any changes to either or any aircraft was done by

both Army and Marines in committee, and had to be approved by both. The only difference in the aircraft was the tail number [serial number].

"Another difference was that for backup support, i.e. maintenance, or extra passengers such as Congressmen on trips we used the Army Boeing CH-47 Chinook and the Marines used the Sikorsky CH-53.

"Those Helicopters were Navy aircraft and were provided in the Navy budget," Downing remembers. "For a time, the Military Aide to the President was a Navy admiral. The Marines from HMX-1 [the presidential flying squadron, nicknamed the 'Nighthawks'] had a full-time Liaison Officer in the White House and there was considerable pressure to give the entire mission to the Marines. I have always believed that these factors were a big part of making the decision [in 1976] to close the Army Flight Detachment and turn the helicopter mission exclusively to the Marines. Since the Army has always been the major user of helicopters and has vastly more experience in Rotary wing aircraft, I have always been of the opinion that this was a more appropriate job for the Army. Apparently the Pentagon doesn't agree."

During the Eisenhower, Kennedy, and Johnson years, a fleet of helicopters stood ready to evacuate the president and other high-ranking officials from Washington on short notice. Initially, these were Sikorsky H-19s, replaced by Piasecki H-21Bs like the one shown here (aircraft no. 52-8701) undergoing noise evaluation tests at Andrews Air Force Base, Maryland. These were not presidential aircraft and in fact never carried a president, but they remained prepared to do so, around the clock. *Frank C. Fox*

Wearing one of his trademark cardigan sweaters—part of his effort to make the presidency less regal—President Jimmy Carter conducts official business aboard Air Force One. President Carter ordered that the "V" designation be removed from the VC-137C aircraft, after which time it became simply a C-137C. This photograph was taken in 1978. *Courtesy of the National Archives*

FORD AND CARTER

Gerald Ford became the nation's 38th president on August 9, 1974, when Nixon resigned over the Watergate scandal. After Army One flew him to Andrews on his last day in office, Nixon departed for California aboard SAM 27000. At the time of takeoff, the aircraft used the call sign Air Force One. The aircraft was approaching the Mississippi River when the hour of noon arrived and Gerald Ford's new job became official. (No president had resigned before and none has since. The Constitution does not prescribe how it should occur, and the decision to make it happen at noon was Nixon's.) As the flight continued westward, the Federal Aviation Administration's Kansas City Air Control received the following radio transmission: "Kansas City this is former Air Force One, please change our call sign to SAM 27000." No longer president, Nixon continued his flight to California.

Ford's place in the history of presidential air travel consisted foremost of a bum rap: He sometimes misspoke and appeared awkward, so the press

With First Lady Rosalyn and daughter Amy, President Carter debarks Air Force One in Washington. The family was returning from a visit to Plains, Georgia, the president's home, in 1977. *Courtesy of the National Archives*

President Jimmy Carter (center, behind foreign policy advisor Cyrus Vance at microphone) wanted the presidential fleet to look less ostentatious. He ordered the "V" (for VIP) removed as a prefix to aircraft designations. In this February 18, 1979, snapshot at Andrews, other Carter administration officials are in view, including National Security Advisor Zbigniew Brzezinski at left with gloves, yellowish jacket, and fur collar. *Robert F. Dorr*

Vice President George Bush and Chief Master Sergeant Kenneth Witkin aboard Air Force Two, circa 1986. The airborne communications systems operator (ACSO) has a crucial job aboard a presidential or vice-presidential aircraft. Witkin was an Air Force communicator for 30 years and finished his military career flying on Bush's aircraft during the Reagan administrations. *White House*

gave Ford a reputation for bumping his head on his helicopter doorway. In fact, it happened only once and its significance was vastly overstated. In a famous utterance that has been quoted incorrectly by the press for decades, Lyndon Johnson had dismissed Ford as "a man who can't chew gum and fart at the same time," but though Ford was also photographed stumbling when boarding SAM 27000, he was, in fact, neither physically nor socially awkward. The rep was unfair.

While campaigning for the nation's highest office in 1976, Georgia Governor Jimmy Carter traveled in a Boeing 727 dubbed *Peanut One*. After Ford's 30-month tenure, Carter became the 39th U.S. president on January 20, 1977. Even before he took office, *Time* magazine wrote of his wish to make the presidency less regal: "He wants to minimize the use of Air Force One and to ride in an armored Ford LTD instead of the bigger and fancier Continental limousine most Presidents have used."

This VC-137B Stratoliner (68-6971) is departing the E-Systems facility in Greenville, Texas following modification work, circa 1985. This aircraft had just completed an extensive overhaul and repainting, and was returning to presidential duty. Number 68-6971 has since been scrapped. During its career, it was a backup presidential aircraft. *Air Force*

With its American flag pointing stars fore, as custom requires, this VC-137 takes off at a 1976 air show at Andrews Air Force Base, Maryland. Note how the blue trim no longer passes over the top of the cockpit as it did on earlier Air Force One paint schemes. *Courtesy of the National Archives*

The presidential VC-137C was the first aircraft to have a communications suite with space for more than one operator. This is the final communications console on the final VC-137C (72-7000, or "SAM 27000," which was finally retired only in 2001 after flying more presidential miles than any other aircraft). The console was built by E-Systems of Greenville, Texas, and utilizes a Collins switching system and Collins high frequency (HF) and very high frequency/ultra high frequency (VHF/UHF) radios. At the start of 2001, no longer given presidential duties, 72-7000 was the only VC-137 left in service. Three VC-137Bs had been retired (two of them scrapped) and the other VC-137C resided at the Air Force Museum in Dayton, Ohio. *Air Force*

Although aircrews remembered Carter as gentlemanly and pleasant, he seemed in many ways an adversary to those who maintained and flew Air Force One. Several sources confirm that Carter exasperated radio operators by discussing classified material "in the open" on the airwaves—although this is very much a president's prerogative.

Carter ordered the "V" prefixed on governmental aircraft designations removed, so SAM 27000, no longer a VC-137C, became merely a C-137C. The same change was made with other VIP aircraft at Andrews. Carter also ordered a toning-down of the markings on Air Force One and other VIP transports.

Carter was viewed as lively and exciting by crew members, especially those who had flown Nixon and Ford. On flights aboard SAM 27000, Carter sometimes danced in the aisles, sang favorite songs, or popped Bob Dylan into the music system.

Carter's paring-down of the visibility of Air Force One did not last long. Ronald Reagan undid all of it when he took office as the 40th U.S. president on January 20, 1981. Reagan also restored the 'V' prefixes to all of the transports at Andrews.

A version of the KC-135 Stratotanker air-refueling aircraft, the VC-135B (Boeing 717) was never assigned presidential duty, but served with the 89th Wing as an executive transport for other government bigwigs. Although this photo appears to show a model or an artist's conception, it actually depicts a real aircraft, reflecting one of the various attempts to "tone down" the VIP fleet. This VC-135B (62-4127) is in a special paint scheme done by E-Systems in an attempt to give the aircraft a less military look. The year is 1983 or 1984. When Lieutenant General Brent Scowcroft, the White House national security advisor, saw the paint scheme, he ordered an immediate return to the traditional colors. *Air Force*

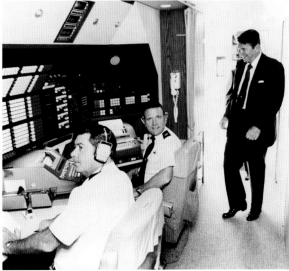

President Ronald Reagan oversees communications systems operators, or CSOs, Chief Master Sergeant Jim Bull (left) and Senior Master Sergeant Jerry Rankin. This is the communications unit aboard the last serving VC-137C, or Boeing 707-353B (72-7000). After serving as Air Force One during the Reagan years, this aircraft was still on duty in 2001. It was during the Reagan years that "radio operators" became CSOs. *White House*

A NEW PRESIDENTIAL AIRCRAFT

The president's plane was late. There was consternation in the nation's capital. "We're very concerned," said Mike Wallace, a civilian spokesman for the Air Force. The focus, fortunately, was not on any aircraft wending its way through the sky, but, rather, on a long-anticipated "high-tech jet" (as the *Washington Times* called it) that was late showing up because it hadn't rolled out of the factory door quite yet.

The president's plane was still being built. It was June 1989, more than 15 months after the "new, gee-whiz Air Force One" (the *Times*, again) was supposed to have been made available for Ronald Reagan. For five months now there had been a new president, George Bush, who was sure to like the new plane. In fact, said one

This 1992 view from the tower at Andrews Air Force Base, Maryland, appears to show maintenance people checking the oil on the number one engine (at the viewer's far left) and washing the windshield (from the cherry picker at right) of Air Force One. In fact, more is going on. The presidential aircraft need to be both safe and clean, and ground crews check them constantly. Normally, however, this kind of work is done indoors and away from prying eyes. This aircraft is "tail number" 29000. *Jim Kippen*

Ronald Reagan, the 40th president of the United States from 1981 to 1989, was supposed to be the first chief executive carried by the new jetliner being customized for White House travel. It did not happen. Reagan finished his eight-year term and returned to California without ever enjoying the copious accommodations of the presidential Boeing 747. *White House*

newspaper account, Bush, "a former naval pilot, will surely delight in its collection of frills and techno-toys." But not yet. There were going to be further delays, Wallace told the author of this volume. "It looks like we probably won't be able to deliver the new Air Force One until some time in 1990," he said prophetically.

The secret behind the delay, or so the public was told, was a last-minute requirement that the electrical veins and arteries of the Boeing 747-200B, or VC-25A in Air Force jargon, be "hard-wired" to resist EMP, or electromagnetic pulse.

An invisible byproduct of a nuclear explosion, EMP can fry a computer chip, battery, or electrical wire not insulated against its onslaught. But insulation adds weight, and weight can slow down an aircraft, or degrade its performance. Raise the weight of a new aircraft by too many pounds and it will not fly at all. In Wichita, Boeing's Carolyn Russell announced that the problem was "being addressed"—and it was. The finished VC-25A sacrificed weight elsewhere and came in at the original expected gross weight of 836,000 pounds.

Was the EMP issue a last-minute hang-up, or merely the public excuse for a delay caused by many

factors? A delay in meeting a military aircraft delivery schedule is hardly unusual, especially when the aircraft (in this case) has six million parts. The process of hardening some buildings, warships, and aircraft against EMP dated to the mid-1960s, and it strains credibility that EMP hardening was not part of the original requirement for the new Air Force One. More likely, the delay was simply a delay, a routine one interpreted with undue harshness by a press unversed in how planes are designed, developed, built, and fielded.

SELECTING THE NEW PLANE

The decision to pick a new plane for the president was difficult. Among those on Capitol Hill who keep their clutch on the purse strings, some feared that the public would see a new plane as wasteful and ostentatious. Others thought it would be a waste of money unless it was purchased in their district. But while the decision process was arduous, most in Washington took the choice of aircraft type for granted almost from the beginning.

It would be a 747 or nothing.

Among robust, wide-bodied jets with a "Made in U.S.A." label, only the 747 was still in production at a cost and rate that made sense to a prospective buyer. The 747 was, after all, the standard against which every other large transport was measured, then and now.

When the 747 ushered in the wide-body era in the 1970s ("jumbo jets," the ads called them), three American companies were building large airliners. Boeing and Douglas were the best known. The third was Lockheed, maker of the L-1011 TriStar, an airliner with a good reputation for reliability that was less familiar to the public than the Boeing 747 or Douglas DC-10.

Lockheed had once been in the big league among airline manufacturers. The Constellation—a fetching, four-engine, propeller-driven craft of the 1940s and 1950s—is regarded as one of the most graceful and majestic machines ever to take to the sky. But since production of the turboprop

Electra ended in 1962, Lockheed had gone for years without building an airliner. Viewed in retrospect, the L-1011 TriStar seems to have been a kind of last gasp.

Developed in Palmdale, California, by a design team headed by William M. Hannan, the TriStar was the laggard among the trio of wide-body jets. The L-1011 made its first flight on November 17, 1970, a late debut compared with February 9, 1969, for the 747 and August 29, 1970, for the Douglas DC-10. Lockheed's wide-body airliner was launched just as the company faced crippling delays with its C-5 Galaxy transport for the Air Force. The TriStar itself was similarly delayed when its own engine configuration ran into technical problems. The L-1011 did not make its first revenue flight (wearing the blue and white colors of

Eastern Air Lines) until April 26, 1972, a milestone that had been easily surpassed by the 747 on January 22, 1970, and the DC-10 on August 5, 1971.

TRISTAR POWER

The TriStar suffered teething troubles, principally with its 48,000-pound-thrust Rolls-Royce RB211-524 turbofan engines that had to be taken out of service for inspection at very frequent intervals. But apart from these comparatively short-term problems, Lockheed's wide-body transport demonstrated efficient operation. It impressed operators, passengers, and the public with its reliability and with the low noise-levels of the Rolls engines.

The L-1011 TriStar had a wing span of 155 feet 4 inches, weighed 477,000 pounds when fully loaded, and offered a 19-foot 7-inch fuselage

The L-1011 TriStar, seen here in an advanced version proposed to the airlines in the late 1970s, was always a potential contender for the Air Force One mission. When decision time came, the L-1011 was no longer in production, but thought was given to refurbishing used models. A superb aircraft that never received the recognition it deserved, the L-1011 joined the 747 and DC-8 in ushering-in the wide-body age. But the Air Force wanted four engines. *Lockheed*

Of the three wide-body, or "jumbo jet" transports that came into use in the 1970s, the Douglas DC-10 was the second best-known, sometimes overshadowed by the 747 but very much respected in its own right. This artist's conception, released by Douglas in about 1980, asks the viewer to imagine what an Air Force One based upon the DC-10 would have looked like. Douglas later manufactured KC-10 Extender tanker/transports, but the company's vision of transporting the president never reached fulfillment. *Douglas*

width, permitting an internal cabin width up to 18 feet 11 inches. There was nothing about the size and shape of this aircraft to make it anything other than a prime candidate for the president. In fact, one user in the Middle East had purchased an L-1011 TriStar and had spent more money plushing-up the interior of the aircraft than the price tag of the plane itself. Moreover, there was a firm precedent for using the L-1011 as a military craft: Britain's Royal Air Force acquired nine of the planes for a dual mission as tankers and transports.

Lockheed eventually manufactured 250 TriStars. There was a short period when developmental problems with the DC-10 gave Lockheed an edge (and a slot in second place, when competing with the 747) but it was a brief moment in the sun.

By the 1980s when the Pentagon's requirement for a new presidential aircraft was taking serious shape, Lockheed was no longer building L-1011s. Foreshadowing a future in which competition would be even further reduced, the number of makers of "jumbo jets" had dropped to two.

Presidential Candidate?

Lockheed's Jeff Rhodes remembers it a different way: "Did Lockheed want to propose an aircraft for Air Force One? No. Because the requirement called for a four-engined airplane. There was some talk at the time that McDonnell Douglas would submit a DC-10. But the specification that came out from the Air Force called for a four-engined aircraft, which kind of leveled the playing field. The only thing we could have offered at the time was a refurbished, redone L-1011 because they were no longer in production. It was supposed to be in time for Reagan to fly back to California, so that would have been [January 1989], but the L-1011 went out of production in 1982. So we wouldn't have had a new airplane."

Nevertheless, some in southern California—still, in those days, the center of the aviation industry, although its relentless decline had already begun—remember that Lockheed was serious about wanting to see Ronald Reagan in an L-1011.

"By the time the Air Force requirement gelled, we were no longer building L-1011s," remembers Frederick Newman, who worked at the manufacturer's Burbank, California, headquarters. "But there were airframes around with relatively few flying hours and we felt we could fix up a couple of them to meet presidential standards. We were not going to concede the playing field to the Boeing 747 without some effort on our part."

Apparently, the Pentagon re-shaped the playing field with its four-engine requirement, and Lockheed's role never progressed beyond the planning stage.

DOUGLAS ENTRY

The story may have been slightly different in Long Beach, California, where Douglas Aircraft was one of the nation's premier builders of transports. In the mid-1980s when a new aircraft for the president was being pondered, Douglas had been, since 1966, a component of the larger McDonnell Douglas Corporation but had very much retained its separate identity as the manufacture of the famous DC series of airliners, including the DC-3, the most famous flying machines of all, and the DC-8, one of the first jetliners. Douglas' entry into the wide-body, or jumbo jet, era, the DC-10, was in many ways as well known and as much admired as the 747.

Douglas viewed the historic advent of the 747 with caution. The southern California manufacturer, which had been acquired by McDonnell in 1966, forged ahead with the DC-10 with both American Airlines and United Airlines as launch customers. When the first DC-10 revenue flight was made by American on August 5, 1971, Douglas had taken just three years and four months between the decision to begin production and entry into scheduled service. This compares with three years and six months for the 747 (which came first because work was started earlier) and three years and nine months for the L-1011 TriStar.

The typical DC-10 airliner was powered by three 52,500-pound-thrust General Electric CF6-50C1 or -50C2 turbofans. The whale-shaped DC-10 was 182 feet 1 inch long with a wingspan of 165 feet 4-1/2 inches. Maximum take-off weight was 572,000 pounds. The wide-body seating was greeted with enthusiasm by travelers and caused one in-flight magazine to run an article on "A Revolution in How We Carry People."

Competitors in the sky. In this air-refueling link-up, the tanker at left is the KC-10A Extender, military version of the Douglas DC-1030CF, which the Air Force chose in preference to the 747 for a 60-plane military purchase in the 1970s. At right is the first military 747, the Boeing E-4A "Doomsday plane," or NEACP (pronounced "Kneecap," for National Emergency Airborne Command Post). Seen in its original configuration without an equipment "hump" behind the flight deck, the E-4A subsequently was modified to become the E-4B NAOC (National Airborne Operations Center). According to one source, crews of Air Force One today still use the E-4B for air-refueling practice as often as possible, because they are leery of scratching the paint on the nose of the VC-25A, which has its refueling receptacle in the same location. *Dept. of Defense*

Following spread: The winner—the VC-25A. Today, the shape of the "flying White House" has become familiar. A refueling receptacle gives the VC-25A a slight "hump" on the nose not found on other 747s. The communications antennas atop the fuselage exceed in number those of any airline 747. The now-familiar paint scheme is immaculate. This is today's VC-25A, Air Force One. But it did not begin that way. When the aircraft was first built, it was "green" (unpainted) and was flown from the Everett, Washington, factory to Wichita, Kansas, for installation of internal equipment. *Barry Roop*

Military DC-10

Any prospect that the DC-10 might be a candidate for presidential travel was enhanced when the Air Force ordered 60 military versions for a dual role as tanker/transports.

The Douglas KC-10A Extender tanker/transport, an off-the-shelf version of the DC-10-30CF airliner, was acquired to fill the Air Force's need—identified during Operation Nickel Grass, the U.S. airlift to Israel during the October 1973 war—for a dual-role Advanced Tanker/Cargo Aircraft (ATCA).

The United States emphasis on rapid deployment forces in the late 1970s coincided with development of this long-range transport able to haul people and equipment while also functioning as a tanker. In the 1990s, the KC-10 fleet helped the USAF field an expeditionary force to deploy rapidly from U.S. bases to Third World trouble spots.

The KC-10 is a genuine strategic asset with its capability to carry a full payload of 169,409 pounds over a range of 4,370 miles, and its facility to be refueled in flight. The value of this tanker/transport is

demonstrated when a fighter deploys overseas, with the KC-10 carrying support equipment and personnel whilst also refueling the fighters en route.

For the tanker role, the lower section of the KC-10A fuselage is fitted with bladder fuel cells increasing maximum usable fuel to 54,455 U.S. gallons. A boom operator's station is located beneath the rear fuselage where the operator sits in an aft-facing crew seat. A Douglas Advanced Aerial Refueling Boom (AARB) is located on the centerline further aft of the fuselage with a refueling hose reel unit installed adjacently. This arrangement permits single-point refueling of USAF aircraft (with the boom) or US Navy/Marine aircraft (with the hose).

The first flight of a KC-10A took place on July 10, 1980, and its first air refueling on October 30, 1980, with a C-5 as the receiver aircraft. It was the following year that the Air Force began to ponder its new presidential aircraft. Douglas, now closely linked to the Air Force because of the KC-10 order, wanted the job. In Long Beach, California, Douglas proposed a luxury version of its DC-10 airliner.

ADVANTAGE 747

To understand why Boeing had such an advantage with the 747, we need to look at how this great aircraft transformed airline travel. So we now drop back to the mid-1960s, when the first jumbo jet was still a concept in the minds of officials at the Seattle company. Not everyone at that time was sold on the concept. When it first became clear that Boeing was working on a giant, wide-body, turbo-fan-powered long range airliner, scaremongers warned that an aircraft accident might now involve up to 500 lives, while air traffic controllers celebrated an increased carrying capacity that would surely reduce the number of flights and make their job easier. The controllers' celebration overlooked a plain fact that was not yet solidly in evidence. The 747 almost single-handedly opened up air travel to everyone. Far from reducing the number of flights (though it caused a sharp reduction in the number of cross-country bus trips), the 747 was the force

that brought millions into the fuselage and increased flights dramatically.

The 747 resulted from negotiations between Boeing's William Allen and Pan American Airways' Juan Trippe. Pleased with the established track record of the Boeing 707, Trippe wanted a bigger aircraft that would save 30 to 35 percent per seat mile. This would bring lower fares and cargo rates, giving Pan American Airways an edge over the competition. Possibly, he did not fully grasp that he was launching a revolution. On April 13, 1966, Trippe signed a contract for $525 million for 25 aircraft able to carry 350 to 400 passengers. This record order was a shot in the arm for Boeing, which was abruptly delivered from financial worries while free to launch an epoch-making aircraft.

At Boeing's new factory adjacent to Paine Field in Everett, Washington, the manufacturer devoted 14,000 hours of wind tunnel testing to a variety of models, even after metal was cut and the first plane was being built. The company devoted 10 million engineering employee hours on the project. Far from being born overnight, the 747 underwent four years of continuous testing in areas ranging from metal selection to systems operation.

On February 9, 1969, with pilot Jack Waddell in command, the first 747 lifted into the sky over Seattle. Co-pilot Brien Wygle and flight engineer Jess Wallick were also along on the maiden flight. Months later, after delays due to engine problems were resolved, Pan American's Najeeb Halaby, who replaced Trippe, used his own test-pilot credentials to personally wring out the 747 and pronounced it the safest, most comfortable, and most magnificently-made plane in history.

Even the crucial milestone of its first revenue flight on January 21, 1970, number crunchers wrote of the 747 in superlatives. When a 747 is fully pressurized, nearly a ton of air is added to its weight. A 747 has 6 million parts. Its tail height of 63 feet 8 inches is equivalent to a six-story building. The wing area of today's 747-400 model is

5,600 square feet an area large enough to hold 45 medium-sized automobiles.

In 1965, only seven percent of Americans had had the experience of traveling aboard an aircraft. By 1982, when the Pentagon was looking for a new Air Force One, the figure was rising toward 40 percent. Today, it is well above 75 percent. The widebody revolution introduced by the 747, accompanied by the DC-10 and L-1011, transformed our lives as did no other event in aviation history. Small wonder that polls consistently make the 747 one of the "most recognized" aircraft in history.

MILITARY 747

Boeing's Everett factory became the 747 Division of Boeing, with John Steiner named vice president for production development. The focus was centered on the airlines, but from the start, Boeing officials also saw military applications for the aircraft.

In 1973, Boeing proposed a version of the 747-200F to the Air Force for consideration as an Advanced Tanker /Cargo Aircraft (ATCA). To sell the proposal, Boeing modified the prototype 747 to perform dry aerial refueling linkups with a nonfunctioning flying boom apparatus. Boeing missed

The Air Force's other 747 in its current configuration. Built as an E-4A, the flying command post is now designated E-4B and is called the NAOC (National Airborne Operations Center). With the end of the Cold War and the delivery of the VC-25A with its modern communications suite, the E-4B has now become largely a backup in its "Doomsday" role. But it could still fill in for the VC-25A as a flying command post for the president in wartime. *Jim Kippen*

The first VC-25A was completed at the manufacturer's facility in Everett, Washington, and flown to the Wichita, Kansas, plant to be fitted with internal equipment. During this period in late 1989 and early 1990, it was a "green airplane," not yet attired in Air Force markings. The green color is in the metal's alloy and is known as anodizing. It is a protective process. When you see a polished silver section, it is generally covered with what is known as Alclad, and that is more of a pure aluminum. It is also more expensive than the alloys. However, the alloys need protection, and the anodization process essentially keeps the aluminum from oxidizing. *Dept. of Defense*

a chance for a lucrative 747 military order, however, when the Air Force chose the KC-10 Extender, the tanker-transport version of the Douglas DC-10 instead of the 747.

Boeing had better luck when the Air Force went shopping for a "Doomsday Plane." In 1973, the Air Force selected the 747-200 as its E-4A Advanced Airborne National Command Post (AABNCP). Subsequently known as the National Emergency Airborne Command Post (NEACP, pronounced "Kneecap,"), the E-4A's job was to provide an aerial command center for the U.S. leadership in wartime. For years, it was kept at Andrews Air Force Base on constant alert to carry the president, or others in the chain of leadership known as the National Command Authority (NCA), during the initial hours or days of a general conflict. During an attack on U.S. soil, some leaders would be taken to an underground command post in Virginia while others would go aboard the E-4B to direct American forces.

Three E-4s (Air Force serial numbers 73-1676/1677 and 74-0787) were delivered in July 1973, October 1973, and October 1984. After a brief period with interim powerplants, they were powered by four General Electric F103-GE-100 turbofan engines. A fourth aircraft (75-0125) was delivered in August 1975 as the E-4B model with significantly improved avionics and communications equipment. The three earlier aircraft were subsequently brought up to E-4B standard. During the years when Jimmy Carter was president (1977–1981), their mission was de-emphasized and they were transferred to the 55th Wing at Offutt Air Force Base, Nebraska, although they still appear frequently at Andrews.

Doomsday Plane

Modified extensively in the years after it was introduced, the E-4B was meant to accommodate the president (in his role as commander in chief of U.S. forces) and key members of his battle staff on its vast main deck, partitioned into five operating compartments. These are the flight crew section, the National Command Authority (NCA) area (roughly a flying equivalent of the White House Situation Room), a conference room, battle staff, and C3I (command, control, communications, and intelligence) area. A second deck provides a rest area for mission personnel.

This "war readiness aircraft" is equipped with nuclear thermal shielding, low frequency/very low frequency (LF/VLF) radios, and extensive satellite communications equipment. Included is equipment to tie into commercial telephone and radio networks to broadcast emergency messages to the general population. The E-4B is distinguished from the original model by its super high frequency (SHF) system with antennas housed in a distinctive blister above and behind the flight deck. Every component of the aircraft, including engines, avionics, and wiring has been optimized for maximum flight duration. The E-4B's sustainability aloft is limited only by oil lubricant of its engines.

The E-4B is now identified by the term National Airborne Operations Center (NAOC) and has been given new duties, including support in federal emergencies such as floods and forest fires. Some sources say that it is no longer needed in the "Doomsday role" because of the advance communications suite aboard the VC-25A (the current Air Force One), but at least one E-4B remains on some degree of alert to become the commander-in-chief's battle headquarters if necessary.

PRESIDENTIAL 747

In July 1986, the Air Force finally placed an order with Boeing for two presidential 747s. The White House had wanted the 747s on duty in time to carry the 40th president, Ronald Reagan, home to California when Reagan left office in January 1989. Delivery of the airplanes was delayed, however, and the 747s did not carry a president until September 6, 1990, when George Bush was in office.

As mentioned previously, the delays in completing the two 747s received considerable attention in the late 1980s. The aircraft were built at the

Green monster. Photographer Alex Hrapunov was attending a reunion of the F-4 Phantom Society at McConnell Air Force Base near Wichita, Kansas, in March 1990 when he looked above a Phantom to see a giant green 747 making "touch and go" landings. Sunlight was sparse, the distance was considerable, and the resulting picture was a little blurred, but it turned out to be a dramatic shot of the soon-to-be Air Force One undergoing early flight tests while being fitted out in Wichita. *Alex Hrapunov*

Boeing plant in Everett, Washington, and were flown in unfinished (green) configuration to the maker's facility in Wichita, Kansas. Here, the problems arose. The Associated Press attributed the problem to "doomsday technology"—the hardening of internal wiring and systems against EMP. But the need to harden the aircraft against EMP had been seen from the beginning. The real reason for the delay was a more general problem integrating systems. By one account, this added $400 million to the original $261 million price for the two 747s, with the manufacturer picking up the tab.

Meanwhile, the press carped. The *Washington Times'* Frank Murray complained beneath the headline "Bush's high-jet jet delayed once again." The first of the two 747s was "already 15 months late," Murray grumbled in June 1989. The reporter wondered whether Bush would "ever get to use the new 747."

Eventually, however, modifications to the first aircraft were completed and it retraced the route from Wichita to Everett to be painted. The 89th Wing took delivery of the first craft on August 23, 1990. The second ship followed it on December 20, 1990.

The two aircraft (constructor's numbers 23824 and 23825) originally received Air Force serial numbers 86-8800 and 86-8900, reflecting their purchase in fiscal year 1986, but soon after delivery were renumbered 82-8000 and 92-8000 to be more in keeping with the numbers used on the VC-137s (62-6000 and 72-7000). This made it possible to give four successive presidential aircraft numbers that could be arranged in sequence—SAM 26000, 27000, 28000, and 29000. The aircraft also temporarily wore Federal Aviation Administration civil registry numbers while being flown by Boeing crews before being turned over to the Air Force.

As part of its preparations to receive the new (and delayed) flying White House, on January 20, 1989, the 89th Airlift Wing named Colonel Robert C. "Danny" Barr presidential pilot, replacing Colonel Robert E. Ruddick. It was no coincidence than this was inauguration day, or that George

Being test-flown by company pilots at Mc-Connell Air Force Base near Wichita, Kansas on March 30, 1990, the first of two VC-25As is still in "green" configuration nearly three years after its first flight on May 16, 1987. Although the aircraft wears no distinctive markings to reveal its identity, the row of antennas atop the fuselage is a sure sign that this is no ordinary 747 airliner. At this point in time, the first aircraft was still nearly five months away from its delivery to the Air Force in August. Total time between first flight and delivery to the 89th Airlift Wing: 39 months. *Sunil Gupta*

This makes it official. Wearing safety harnesses as they work high up on the side of the airplane, Boeing employees apply the presidential seal decal to the new Air Force One. *Boeing via Tom Kaminski*

The Green Machine

At the end of March 1990 (five months before it was delivered to the Air Force), the first VC-25A, still green and sporting "N6005C" in a white rectangle on its fin, was conducting flight tests at Wichita. The aircraft was flying from the manufacturer's side of the airfield, which is co-located with McConnell Air Force Base. No publicity attended these flight tests, and they received little notice in the press, although the occasional story could be found reporting that both planes were delayed.

The term "green" has come to refer to an airplane that has not yet been completed, but in this case it had a literal meaning as well. In order to protect the polished silver aluminum covering the VC-25A, the airplane was covered with an alloy, which is a more-pure aluminum and which makes the airplane look green. The alloy covering essentially keeps the aluminum from oxidizing.

Among observers who witnessed the president's aircraft flying at Wichita were several dozen members of the F-4 Phantom Society, who were holding a reunion, called a "Phancon" at McConnell. For the occasion, the Air Force side of the field was populated with F-4 Phantom fighters visiting from several units.

Jeff Rankin-Lowe, one of the participants, looked at the big green 747 with considerable interest. "It caught most of us by surprise," Lowe remembered a decade later, "as we were absorbed with a ramp full of 50 Phantoms and the metallic green color of the 747 was unexpected for many of us [who were] perhaps more used to zinc chromate primer. The speculation was that it was one of the 'Air Force One' aircraft but no one knew for sure at the time." Another participant said he knew "exactly what it was" and believed civilian test pilots were doing the flying. "While we were there," the second participant said, "the aircraft remained on the [manufacturer's] ramp. It never once entered an Air Force part of the field except when necessary to land and take off."

The manufacturer's records list the first flight of the VC-25A as January 26, 1990, in Wichita, an apparent reference to a proving flight that took

Bush was taking office as the 41st chief executive. While the president's chief pilot is chosen for experience, integrity, and ability, it is often left to the White House to choose the head of the presidential pilot's office. Barr and other pilots working with him became the first to receive training to fly the VC-25A, initially in a simulator at Everett. It is unclear, however, whether they were exposed to the actual aircraft while fitting work at Wichita was still taking place.

The first of two presidential 747 (VC-25A) transports, in green configuration, is brought into the hangar at Wichita, Kansas, for outfitting to bring the aircraft up to standard for White House use. Note that the engine intakes are covered; the plane is being towed by a tractor. Both aircraft were manufactured in Everett, Washington, brought to Wichita for interior work, then returned to Everett for painting. *Boeing via Tom Kaminski*

Back at the factory in Everett, home of all 747 models, a presidential 747 (VC-25A) is being transformed into Air Force One. A Boeing employee completes the finishing touches on decal letters spelling "UNITED STATES OF AMERICA" on the side of the fuselage. Painting the aircraft in Air Force markings was the final step before delivery of the first ship in August 1990. *Boeing via Tom Kaminski*

place nearly three years after the real first flight. The first VC-25A was formally accepted by the Air Force on August 23, 1990. As we shall see, it began flying President Bush almost immediately. The second aircraft was delivered on December 20, 1990.

QUEENIE TO PASTURE

In a ceremony at Andrews on June 14, 1993, the Air Force finally retired *Queenie*—the most presidential of almost-presidential aircraft—after nearly a quarter-century of service. *Queenie* had joined the Air Force on June 12, 1959, as a VC-137A. The Air

Force never earmarked *Queenie* for presidential duty, but she served as a backup to Air Force One (alias SAM 26000) for a decade. *Queenie* also carried Henry Kissinger to China to begin President Richard Nixon's dramatic rapprochement with that country in 1972. Moreover, *Queenie* was the first jet-propelled aircraft in the Air Force inventory specifically intended for the transport of personnel. Every previous jet had been designed to carry guns, bombs, or fuel.

Queenie carried American chief executives on numerous travels beginning August 24, 1959,

Built at Everett, modified in Wichita, then returned to Everett for painting, the new Air Force One rolls out of the paint hangar in about July 1990, ready at last to be turned over to the Air Force's 89th Airlift Wing. This is the first photo ever taken of the 747 as it appears in presidential colors. *Boeing via Tom Kaminski*

when Dwight D. Eisenhower on a European trip became the first president to travel by jet. Presidents Kennedy, Johnson, Nixon, and Bush also made travels on the aircraft. *Queenie* was retired to the Museum of Flight in Seattle.

SAM 26000 RETIRES, TOO

While the new 747s were entering service, the Air Force continued to operate its first presidential Boeing 707, otherwise known as SAM 26000. When state-of-the-art communications systems for the new aircraft were being developed, they were first tested on SAM 26000. In 1981, SAM 26000 carried former presidents Nixon, Ford, and Carter to the funeral of Egyptian President Anwar Sadat. In 1983 she carried Queen Elizabeth II on a visit to the west coast of the United States.

On May 20, 1998, after making presidential flights for more than three decades, presidential aircraft SAM 26000 made its final approach into Wright-Patterson Air Force Base, Ohio, to arrive at a permanent resting place at the U.S. Air Force Museum. The VC-137C was greeted by a crowd of well-wishers at a museum ceremony including

The first presidential 747 (VC-25A) arrives on its first trip carrying an occupant of the White House. The location is Topeka, Kansas: the date September 6, 1990. It is George Bush's first foray in the new Air Force One. Even at a considerable distance from home, the 41st president (not shown here) is using a stairway brought to Topeka aboard an Air Force cargo aircraft, rather than the internal "airstairs" of the 747.
Jerry Geer

Major General Charles D. Metcalf, director of the museum; Air Force Materiel Command Commander General George T. Babbitt; and several former crew members.

The aircraft that had served presidents from John F. Kennedy onward was replaced as the primary presidential aircraft by its stablemate SAM 27000 in 1972, and by the twin Boeing 747s in 1990. SAM 2600 continued to serve as a backup presidential aircraft until the day of its final flight. Its companion aircraft, SAM 27000, remained in service for three years longer.

Retired Colonel James Swindall, who piloted SAM 26000 through the Kennedy and Johnson administrations, was a special guest at the museum ceremony. Swindall said the most memorable moment aboard the presidential aircraft was a sad one—the flight back to Washington from Dallas after President Kennedy was assassinated.

The former Air Force One will continue to tell an important part of the Air Force story at the museum, where it will be seen by more than one million visitors each year.

TECHNICAL DESCRIPTION

The 43rd U.S. president, George W. Bush, inherited an aircraft that is well known to the public, especially to movie audiences. Air Force One is the term by which the public recognizes the 747 transport (a pair of them) operated solely for presidential travel by the U.S. Air Force's 89th Airlift Wing at Andrews Air Force Base, Maryland. In actuality, Air Force One is the radio call sign for any Air Force plane carrying the president. For example, the call sign was used for a VC-9C Skytrain II, the military version of the Douglas DC-9, used by President Bill Clinton on one of his final trips as president, to Nebraska, on December 8, 2000. During his second term in office, Clinton also made a brief flight to Bosnia aboard a C-17A Globemaster III, which, for that brief interlude, became Air Force One.

Close to the camera, SAM 29000 makes an arrival at Barksdale Air Force Base, Louisiana, on February 6, 1994. The occasion is a visit by President Bill Clinton. This close to the big military 747, we can see the distinctive "hump" on the nose created by the air refueling receptacle (although there is no public record of the VC-25A flying an air-refueled mission) as well as various antennas for the elaborate communications suite. *Greg L. Davis*

Of course, no president flew aboard more aircraft types than Lyndon Johnson (VC-137B/C, VC-131H, VC-140, VC-6A), and when he was aboard each of these used the call sign as well.

Today even insiders use the term Air Force One in everyday conversation to refer to the pair of presidential 747s at Andrews. Designated VC-25A by the military, they are Boeing 747-200Bs or, in more technical terms, Boeing 747-2G4Bs. Remarkably, although the VC-25A is one of the most readily recognized aircraft in the world—millions saw Harrison Ford, a pilot in real life, fly it in the 1997 movie *Air Force One*—this is the first time a technical

analysis of the aircraft has been published. The details that follow were assembled from open sources without direct assistance by the manufacturer of the airplane or the Air Force.

A BIG PLANE

At the core of the Air Force's decision to purchase the 747 lay a belief that no longer holds much currency. "In the 1980s when we wanted a new presidential aircraft, nobody would hear of anything with less than four engines," says a Pentagon officer. The age of twin-engine, two-pilot airliners had already arrived, but in the Pentagon the Air Staff

insisted that the occupant of the White House needed a jet with four engines and a flight crew consisting of no fewer than four, namely two pilots, a flight engineer, and a navigator. It was as if no progress had been made in aviation for a decade and ETOPS (Extended Twin-Engined Operations, or the loosening of standards for long distance flights) had never happened.

In the late 1960s when every transport aircraft had at least three flight crew members, the 747 forged a unique reputation as the wide-body jetliner that had opened up air travel to the masses. The 747 first flew on February 9, 1969, and made its first passenger revenue flight with Pan American World Airways on January 22, 1970. By the time the Air Force went shopping, Boeing was close to the first flight of its two-pilot 747-400 (on April 26, 1988), which has since become the most numerous version of the famous jet, and was readily producing plenty of 767 airliners (first flight, September 26, 1981), which could span vast distances not only with two pilots but with two engines. The Air Force was hearing none of it.

Douglas, however, heard the Air Staff loud and clear. Between 1978 and 1982, Douglas' Long Beach, California, plant manufactured 60 KC-10

A series of nose-to-tail, close-up views of SAM 28000. *Sunil Gupta*

TECHNICAL DESCRIPTION

Frequently, the president simply walks from the helicopter to the Boeing 747. Presidents rarely get to do anything alone, however. The police vehicle seen here belongs to Air Force Security Forces (known at the time of this photo as Security Police), who handle part of the job of protecting the chief executive and are also responsible for protecting airbases from attack. Not evident in this view is the VC-25A, which is only a short distance to the viewer's right. In the distant background is the Marine Corps Air Reserve facility at Andrews. *Charles Taylor*

The president leaves members of his entourage in the lurch and climbs aboard Air Force One using portable stairs provided by ground services personnel at Andrews (not the self-contained airstairs of the aircraft, which are inside the closed door to the right of the presidential seal). At the point where he waves goodbye to well-wishers, the president is 22 feet above the ground, but still below the level of the pilots on the flight deck who are approximately 24 feet in the air. The aircraft shown is SAM 28000. *Charles Taylor*

Extender tanker/transports. The company aggressively promoted its three-engined DC-10 as the new Air Force One. But Air Force leaders had a tin ear toward any aircraft with fewer than four-engines, and the marketing effort quickly sagged.

Ironically, the Air Force no longer counts engines with such fervor. The 89th Wing at Andrews now operates four twin-engined C-32As (Boeing 757-200) and was scheduled to receive its first twin-engined C-40B (Boeing 737-700) in June 2002. The C-32A frequently carries Vice President Dick Cheney using the call sign Air Force Two. Before the idea was dropped as being too ostentatious, the service was also close to purchasing a handful of 767s, also with twin engines.

Four General Electric F103-GE-180 turbofan engines, better known by their civilian name, CF6-80C2B1, power the presidential 747s. The engines provide 56,750 pounds of thrust, or about the same power as two railroad locomotives operating at maximum throttle. They typify the new age of power, which has given heavies more thrust than

they need. Were it not aerodynamically quite impossible, the thrust available to the VC-25A would easily enable it to fly straight up.

The VC-25A has the standard 747 twin-lobe fuselage. The VC-25A is equipped to receive in-flight refueling via a standard Air Force-style boom receptacle, which slightly changes the shape of the extreme nose ahead of the cockpit. To insure the VC-25A is self-sufficient on the ground, it is equipped with a second Garrett AiResearch GTC331-200 auxiliary power unit in the lower lobe.

ON THE FLIGHT DECK

The cockpit of the VC-25A provides ample room for two pilots, navigator, and flight engineer, and is thus substantially roomier than the flight deck of a comparable airliner.

On today's VC-25A, those crew members belong to the Presidential Airlift Group, known prior to April 1, 2001, as the Presidential Pilot's Office (PPO), but always having the status of an Air Force group under the 89th Wing at Andrews.

The moment its high-stakes passenger is on board (the president usually is last to get on and first to get off), SAM 28000 buttons up and pulls away from the mobile stairway structure...

...turns its backside to the camera...

...and faces no interruption of any kind being cleared for takeoff and launching into the air. *Charles Taylor*

The presidential pilot heads the group. At the start of 2001, that job—equivalent to a group commander at any other base—belonged to Colonel Mark Donnelly, often described as the most experienced 747 pilot in the Air Force. The presidential pilot reports to the commander of the 89th Wing who, at the beginning of 2001, was Brigadier General James Hawkins. The next rung up the ladder is higher headquarters at 21st Air Force, located at McGuire Air Force Base, New Jersey, and commanded at the start of 2001 by Major General George "Nick" Williams. Going still higher, 21st Air Force is part of Air Mobility Command, headed up at this time by General Charles A. "Tony" Robertson. That command arrangement is solidly entrenched, but military life being what it is, Donnelly, Hawkins, and Robertson all moved on to be replaced by new incumbents—presidential pilot Colonel Mark Tillman, 89th Wing commander Colonel Glenn Spears, and AMC commander General John Handy—with only Williams occupying the same role when this volume went to print.

Whoever the presidential pilot happens to be, he looks down at the world from a lofty perch. On the VC-25A, the pilots sit on a flight deck situated fully 29 feet above the ground, roughly 100 feet in front of the main landing gear, and 12 feet in front of the nose gear. Being this high up and this far forward demands careful thinking and a great deal of training, when Air Force One is being maneuvered on the ground. Yet in spite of the enormous size of the VC-25A, the flight deck is essentially the same size as the one on the earlier VC-137C.

In addition to the four flight crew members on the front deck, the VC-25A has crew positions for three ACSOs (airborne communications systems operators), although even on routine missions it carries an extra ACSO for a total of four. In the early days of military flying, a separate crew position was needed on large aircraft to operate the radios, and the first airborne radio operators were drawn from the Army's Signal Corps. Since World War II, radio operators have typically begun their training at Keesler Field, Mississippi, and have been

This angle provides an excellent look at the nose contours of Air Force One. President Bill Clinton, waving farewell during a visit to Patrick Air Force Base, Florida, in June 1996, provides a perspective on the enormous size of the aircraft. Again, this aircraft is SAM 29000, the second presidential VC-25A. *John Gourley*

responsible for the HF (high-frequency), VHF (very high frequency), and UHF (ultra high-frequency) radios found on most transports. A 1982 study for the Pentagon's air staff by Chief Master Sergeant Ken Witkin, a radio operator on then-Vice President George Bush's aircraft, Air Force Two, changed the name of the career field from "airborne radio operator" to ACSO. The ACSOs who serve aboard Air Force One are part of the Presidential Airlift Group and serve under a chief of communications, a job held at the start of 2001 by Chief Master Sergeant Mike Tedford. Under this NCO (noncommissioned officer), the second slot is for a standardization and evaluation ACSO, a job held in 2001 by Chief Master Sergeant Ed Moren. One source says that CSOs serving on Air Force One are usually senior NCOs serving their final assignments before retirement. Some end up working as civilians for the White House Communications Agency, which

is so secret the U.S. government will not acknowledge its existence.

REACHING THE WORLD

The VC-25A has a special communications suite served by its three radio operator positions. The MCS (Mission Communications System) provides for worldwide transmission and reception of both normal and secure communications. The MCS includes multifrequency radios and 85 telephones for air-to-ground, air-to-air, and satellite communications. The airmen working at the radio stations have a huge responsibility for strategic communications, but they also handle prosaic tasks such as showing television and film programming to the president and other dignitaries. Much of the design work on the communications suite was directed not by a corporate executive or a senior officer but by one of the actual operators, Chief Master

Sergeant Jimmy Bull, who preceded Tedford in the top communicator's job.

For more than a decade, the Air Force would not even acknowledge the location of the communications facility on the aircraft, which it now says is located on the upper deck behind the flight crew. Fifty percent greater in size than the suite on the previous presidential aircraft, the MCS suite has far more than the standard communications gear found on other big aircraft. Details must be speculative, since officials will not explain how communications for the president are set up, or what equipment is provided for a "Doomsday" scenario in which the commander-in-chief would be aloft at the outbreak of a war. Official sources will say only that the 747 carries a full suite of communications equipment, much of it installed by the former E-Systems, enabling the president to talk to just about anyone. The communications gear effectively

renders obsolete the Air Force's other Boeing 747 model, the E-4B National Airborne Command Post, operated by the 55th Wing at Offutt Air Force Base, Nebraska. With the communications afforded by the V-25A, the president no longer needs a separate command post in wartime.

It should be noted that in the event of a ballistic missile attack on the United States (a "Doomsday" scenario), Pentagon planning includes sufficient air-refueling tankers to keep Air Force One "tanked" with JP-8 aviation fuel indefinitely. It is believed that extra work was done on the VC-25A's engines to increase the amount of oil available to lubricate them, since this factor—coupled with crew fatigue—would limit the duration the aircraft can stay aloft. Some observers believe the president could be kept airborne for five or six days in the VC-25A with minimal difficulty.

The complex main landing gear of Air Force One comes up while the nose wheel is only beginning its forward retraction. The date is November 4, 1995, the location is Andrews, and the aircraft is SAM 28000.
Joseph G. Handelman

CHAPTER SIX

STUDYING THE INTERIOR

Since the design features of the 747 are well known, it is the interior of the presidential VC-25A that makes Air Force One different. But do not expect a cutaway drawing to emerge from the public affairs shop in Wichita or Seattle. The Air Force not only won't reveal details of the innards of Air Force One (apart from a general description), it won't allow anyone to claim credit for any system or component of the aircraft. In late 2001, the company that makes the MC-1 emergency oxygen mask used by the VC-25A's flight crew, and by no other Air Force heavy, ran an advertisement in *Armed Forces Journal* with a slick painting of the blue and white 747, proclaiming the firm's pride in being associated with the White House's executive jet. The company was requested—by whom is not clear—not to publish the ad again. Everyone associated with Air Force One takes great pride in the aircraft and its systems, and everyone does so in total silence.

Why is it so hard to learn about the interior of Air Force One? As one Air Force officer put it, "They now make a .50-caliber sniper rifle that is accurate to within a square inch at a distance of

The flying Oval Office—literally. As with every passenger seat on the aircraft, those shown here have standard, first-class airline features, including seatbelts. But if the president chooses to stand while the aircraft is taxiing, taking off, or landing, no one will require him to strap in. *Boeing via Tom Kaminski*

The farthest-forward interior compartment of Air Force One, SAM 28000, looking forward, with seats along the fuselage wall. In many respects, the layout is similar to the first-class cabin of Boeing 747 airliners today. Boeing manufactured the VC-25A in Renton, Washington, but did the interior work in Wichita, Kansas. This interior view was released in 1990 and includes ashtrays generously scattered about. Soon afterward, the Air Force issued an instruction banning smoking on all of its aircraft—and transforming into collectors' items the cigarettes that, until then, had been passed out to travelers on the president's plane. *Boeing via Tom Kaminski*

3,000 yards. We don't want that sniper to know exactly where the president sits at his desk." On rare occasions when the press has been exposed to more than the rear passenger compartment—as when *National Geographic* magazine filmed a special on Air Force One—press activity has been closely watched. The Air Force public affairs establishment has tended to provide support (on rare occasion) to "puff pieces" about Air Force One, but not to serious analysis of the aircraft and its mission. The experience of Hollywood movie makers provides a clue to how military bureaucracy and civilian media can clash. When Hollywood asked the Air Force for a guided tour of the inside of Air Force One, according to this same officer, "We said not only no, but hell no." However, months later, while the film was still in preparation, President Bill Clinton had dinner with Harrison Ford at the actor's ranch in Jackson Hole, Wyoming. In a conversational aside that sounded casual but wasn't, Ford asked for a tour of the VC-25A. Clinton instantly agreed to what the Air Force would not. The actor, the film's director, and a handful of staff got their tour. No picture-taking was allowed, but,

Above: This area is known as "the Annex" and is situated close to the conference room. Seen here in executive configuration, it can be converted for use as an emergency medical facility. *Boeing via Tom Kaminski*

Left: The conference room. No cutaway drawing of Air Force One has been released, and no one from the media has been shown the entire aircraft from nose to tail, all part of an effort to keep outsiders from pinpointing the exact location of any particular person, especially the plane's main passenger. This room is located about two-thirds of the way back in the fuselage of the aircraft and has been photographed with a wide-angle lens to make it appear larger than it actually is. This is a 1990 view, and some furnishings have changed since then. *Boeing*

Described as the "staff/secretarial area" when SAM 28000 was first delivered to the Air Force in 1990, this seating area with its fold-down work tables and handy telephones runs across the width of the fuselage near the two-thirds point, just behind the conference room. *Boeing*

This is another view of what was called the "staff/secretarial area" of the current Air Force One in the days before secretaries became associates and most typewriters were replaced with laptops. The location is the right side of the VC-25A near the two-thirds point, just behind the conference room. *Boeing via Tom Kaminski*

as the officer remembers, "They had excellent memories. To a large extent, they accurately reproduced what they saw when they created the movie set."

On the subject of movies, in *Independence Day*, Air Force One arrives at a base where little green men from another galaxy are preserved in glass bottles. And in *Escape from New York*, an especially unpleasant president (the late Donald Pleasance) cheats death by using an escape capsule in which the president can eject from the aircraft in an emergency. Air Force officials will not confirm or deny the little green men, but they are adamant that the VC-25A does not have an escape capsule. Nor are parachutes carried.

REAL-LIFE DRAMA

The real Air Force One has a copious interior. But it is still an aircraft, with limited space, and the Hollywood version is bigger on the inside. The real aircraft includes a presidential suite comprising a conference/dining room, lounge/bedroom, and office space for senior staff members. A second conference room can be converted into a medical

facility, if required. The interior contains work and rest areas for a small presidential staff and a few media representatives, and a rest area for the flight crew. In all, Air Force One provides seating for 70 passengers and 23 crew members.

The VC-25A is equipped with two complete galleys for food preparation, each capable of feeding 50 people. The aircraft has two self-contained "airstairs," aimed at minimizing the need for ground support equipment and permitting the VC-25A to operate with minimal ground support facilities. The self-contained stair units provide entry and exit at a door located below and to the right of the main door, which is normally used for boarding using stairs provided at the air base. A person boarding Air Force One via the "airstairs" would enter in

Powerplant	four General Electric F103-GE-180
	(CF6-80C2B1) turbofan engines providing
	56,750-pounds thrust each
Accommodation:	
flight crew	four (two pilots, navigator, flight engineer)
total crew members	23
normal passenger count	70
Performance:	
maximum level speed	610 miles per hour
cruising altitude	45,000 feet
maximum range	9,100 miles
Weights:	
empty weight	372,500 pounds
maximum take-off weight	793,000 pounds
Dimensions:	
span	195 feet 8 inches
length	231 feet 10 inches
height	63 feet 5 inches

the below-deck storage area and would climb an interior stairway to the main deck. The underfloor storage area is divided into general and special storage locations, the latter including sufficient food for 2,000 meals. The lower deck also contains an automated, self-contained cargo loader and additional equipment.

General Hawkins, former commander of the 89th, remembers when he first saw a VC-25A during an earlier assignment in 1994. "I thought it was a remarkable aircraft," Hawkins said in an interview with the author. "I compared it to the inside of a ship, a cruise ship, with the way it's proportioned, and with the mahogany in the conference room." Hawkins pointed out that while the VC-25A offers comfort suitable for the leader of the most powerful nation in the world, it is by no means opulent or ostentatious: "It is a practical aircraft."

DEFENDING THE VC-25A

The presidential 747 carries no armament. Secret Service agents escorting the president are armed, and their arsenal includes weapons rarely or never seen by the president, including sniper rifles and machine guns. Officials will not discuss the passive or active defensive systems aboard the aircraft, but the VC-25A does have infrared and radar warning devices, chaff, and flares. The pilots operate these from the flight deck.

Details on one such system have come to light. The VC-25A is equipped with the AN/ALQ-204 (MATADOR) infrared (IR) jammer, also known by the program name Have Charcoal—the Air Force's latest defensive weapon against heat-seeking missiles. (The word "Have" identifies the program as developed by Air Force Systems Command). The AN/ALQ-204 is part of a family of IR countermeasures systems de-

29000

To protect Air Force One from heat-seeking missiles, a defensive unit known as the ALQ-204 IRCM (infrared countermeasures) system is installed in the tail of the aircraft, at the very top of the tailcone. An APU (auxiliary power unit) is also located there, down toward the center. The result is a rear-fuselage shape slightly different from that of any other Boeing 747. This aircraft is SAM 29000. *John Gourley*

signed for jet transport and providing coverage for the full 360-degree azimuth surrounding the aircraft. The system consists of multiple transmitters, controller unit, and an operator's controller. The controller unit, which controls and monitors up to two transmitters, electronically synchronizes transmitters.

Each transmitter contains an IR source capability, which emits pulsed radiation to combat multi-IR-guided missiles. Preprogrammed multithreat jamming codes are provided, selectable on the operator's control unit, and all new codes can be entered as required to cope with new threats. (In addition to Air Force One, this defense against infrared missiles equips the Royal Air Force British Aerospace 146 aircraft of the Queen's flight, and 18 other head-of-state or VIP aircraft.)

Maintenance on Air Force One is carried out by enlisted Air Force troops—and not, as at many other Air Force bases, by Air Force or contract civilians. This is unusual, because the rest of the 89th Wing now has shifted to contractor maintenance and uses civilians to keep its planes flying. Like Air Force One's cockpit crew and communicators, the maintenance people belong to the Presidential Airlift Group. The group also operates three C-20C Gulfstream III aircraft. About 1,000 of the 89th Wing's 6,000 members directly support VC-25A operations. The mission seems to be growing. During President Clinton's term (1993–2001), Air Force One touched down in 49 of the 50 U.S. states and 112 countries. During President George W. Bush's first eight months in office, he flew aboard Air Force aircraft more than Clinton did in his first two years.

INTO A NEW CENTURY

Air Force One taxies out of its hangar. Heads turn. No matter how often it happens, everyone within eyesight pauses to gawk as the great flying machine, immaculate in blue, silver, and white, rolls toward the takeoff mark. There is nothing like it in the world.

And it is happening in a one-time forested swamp.

Long ago, when the military built Andrews Air Force Base (then called Camp Springs Army Air Field), they located it far from the nation's capital. If German warplanes appeared overhead at the height of World War II, they might bomb a portion of the base, but it was spread over too much land to make a good target. By being removed from the city, it also spared the city any collateral damage should it come under attack.

SAM 28000 letting down. *Sunil Gupta*

Almost as long ago, when the 89th Airlift Wing (known, in its lifetime, by various names) came to Andrews, it was what the military calls a "tenant unit," one of numerous outfits that inhabit different corners of the installation.

"I remember when things around here seemed normal size," says a senior noncommissioned officer who served at Andrews at the start of a 24-year career and again at the finish. "There's no longer anything normal about this place. The 89th dominates every aspect of this base. This base was once known for a lot of things but today it's known for Air Force One. That's what dominates everything about here, Air Force One."

The German attack that was anticipated when the base was built never came. Washington was abuzz with rumors that a German aircraft carrier had been sighted off the coast of New Jersey—but they contained not a word of truth. Other motives for building Andrews—the active-duty fighter squadrons that defended Washington in the 1950s—have become less important, while the mission of the 89th Wing has become bigger and more vital.

Too, the city has grown out to reach Andrews. Now, the Washington Beltway, otherwise called I-495, runs past the base. Today (though it would have been unthinkable in 1943), some Americans routinely spend two hours or more getting to and from work each day, so Andrews is no longer far from the city, no longer a swamp. In fact, Andrews has become a city in itself.

So, is Air Force One an ambassador of good will, spreading the American message around the globe, winning plenty of goodwill for relatively little cost? Or is Air Force One an excess, overkill, more plane than the presiden needs—a glitzy, pretentious, even ostentatious way of spending the American taxpayer's dollar?

Although the 89th is always sensitive about being perceived as wasteful, the accepted style of presidential travel has never seen serious opposition by Congress, the press, or the public. Most Americans do not want their chief executive traveling in steerage.

The upbeat view of Air Force One is the predominant one. An uplifting, positive view in the 2001 television special by *National Geographic* magazine was heavy on fluff and almost devoid of balance. A more sober version of this upbeat viewpoint was given to the author by Representative Steny Hoyer (D.-Md.), who said, "I believe Air Force One is not there just for the president, but for all the American people. It's there representing all of us. Our freedoms, our culture, our promise for the future, all of it flies every time that airplane

takes off from the ground." Hoyer is now the congressmen for the district where Andrews is located. In 1957, while students at Suitland High School where Andrews-based airmen send their kids, Hoyer and the author skipped school one afternoon to walk to the base and look at airplanes.

There are detractors, of course. In 2000, one presidential trip overseas cost taxpayers $63,442,958 for flights by Air Force One, plus the inevitable but mysterious C-20C Gulfstream III, plus 26 C-5 Galaxys, 33 C-17 Globemaster IIIs,

four C-141s, 10 KC-10s, and one C-130. The trip drew a sharply critical opinion letter in *Air Force* magazine (in January 2001) from Colonel William J. Schwehm. But the criticism sounds different when we remember that the president at the time was Bill Clinton, never popular with military men like Schwehm, and the destination was Vietnam. Although the United States has normal diplomatic relations with Hanoi, many officers, especially war veterans, would criticize any president who traveled there.

Usually kept indoors or at least within the compound that includes their hangar, the two presidential 747s are seen here in front of Base Operations at Andrews. The Andrews control tower is at left, behind the tail of the closer aircraft. *Sunil Gupta*

SAM 28000, the usual 747 employed as Air Force One, in a clean ramp portrait that provides a thorough look at its well-tended exterior. The assortment of antennas running along the upper fuselage is unique to the VC-25A, and Air Force officials prefer not to discuss the purpose of each. Note that when the American flag is displayed on an aircraft, the union (the blue field containing 50 stars) must face forward regardless of which side the flag appears on. *Norris Graser*

CEREMONIAL EVENT

But politics rarely shows its ugly head at Andrews, where members of the 89th Wing are immersed in Air Force culture and immune to the partisan battles that occur on Capitol Hill a few miles away.

Part of that culture, of course, means ceremony.

On April 10, 2001, the national anthem echoes throughout Air Force One's high-ceilinged hangar as glittering VC-25A, C-20, and VC-137C aircraft stand in silent watch over assembled guests. An honor guard raises the flag in front of the VC-25A, alias SAM 29000. Present are civilian dignitaries plus Major General George "Nick" Williams, commander of 21st Air Force; Brigadier General James A. Hawkins, 89th Wing commander; and Colonel Mark Donnelly, the presidential pilot.

The occasion is the formation of the PAG, or Presidential Airlift Group, known for decades as the PPO (Presidential Pilot's Office) but now being renamed and elevated in status. Air Force flight mechanics, communications experts, security forces, and stewards make up the team of over 150 men and women assigned to the PAG.

Williams, as Air Force leaders so often do, utters an upbeat opinion of the VC-25A. "This aircraft is a fitting symbol of our country and its leader," he says.

Williams makes a few observations about the PPO. He explains that the unit has maintained a 100-percent departure reliability rate for over 50 years of safe flying. He mentions that the PPO, now the PAG, has carried over 115,000 passengers for 2.3 million miles.

Hawkins passes the new flag of the PAG to Donnelly, says that much of the presidential transport unit's success is due to Donnelly's efforts, and adds, "Colonel Donnelly always gives all the credit to his troops." Hawkins and Donnelly will both have moved on within a few months, but in the meantime Hawkins adds that the PPO, now the PAG, has always provided "safe, reliable, and comfortable presidential airlift."

The change means that the 89th Airlift Wing will be in the unique position of having two operational groups—the 89th Operations Group, which is responsible for all VIP travel except the president's, and the Presidential Airlift Group. As part of its increased stature, the PAG will oversee a Presidential Airlift Squadron (initially under Major Scott Goodwin) and a Presidential Logistics Squadron (under Major Rodney Davidson).

To most, the change from PPO to PAG is a simple, common-sense acknowledgement that the job of flying the president has grown. To a few, it is a sign that the presidential travel business is becoming more insular. And to Donnelly, who is near the end of his tenure as the latest in a succession of presidential pilots, it is a good deal.

"I'm excited about this change," Donnelly tells the audience at this latest of so many ceremonies held at Andrews. "To all the members of the PAG, thank you for keeping safety, comfort, and reliability at the forefront during this change."

NEW BOSS

Soon after this ceremony, others are held to mark the departure of Donnelly, the presidential pilot, and Hawkins, the wing commander who was on duty during the period this volume was prepared. On June 26, 2001, after 26 years in uniform, Donnelly retires in one of the many ceremonies that are so much a part of daily life at the 89th Airlift Wing. He is the 11th pilot in history to claim the title of primary presidential pilot. Replacing Colonel Robert D. "Danny" Barr, Donnelly got the job on January 20, 1997 (many presidential pilots took up their duties on inauguration day), just over three years after he joined the unit and eight years after arriving at Andrews.

At Donnelly's retirement event, his predecessor Barr makes a revealing comment to the audience: "I often told people that I have a wife and two kids at home." And I always figured that if I got back to them, I would get the president where he wanted to go and back to the White House safely."

During his career, Donnelly has commanded more than 300 flights aboard Air Force One and

Opposite page: With SAM 29000 behind him, Colonel Mark Donnelly stands at a microphone during the formation of the Presidential Airlift Group on April 20, 2001. Seated at right is Major General George "Nick" Williams, commander of 21st Air Force, the numbered air force responsible for operations of the 89th Airlift Wing at Andrews Air Force Base, Maryland. *U.S. Air Force/Bobby Jones*

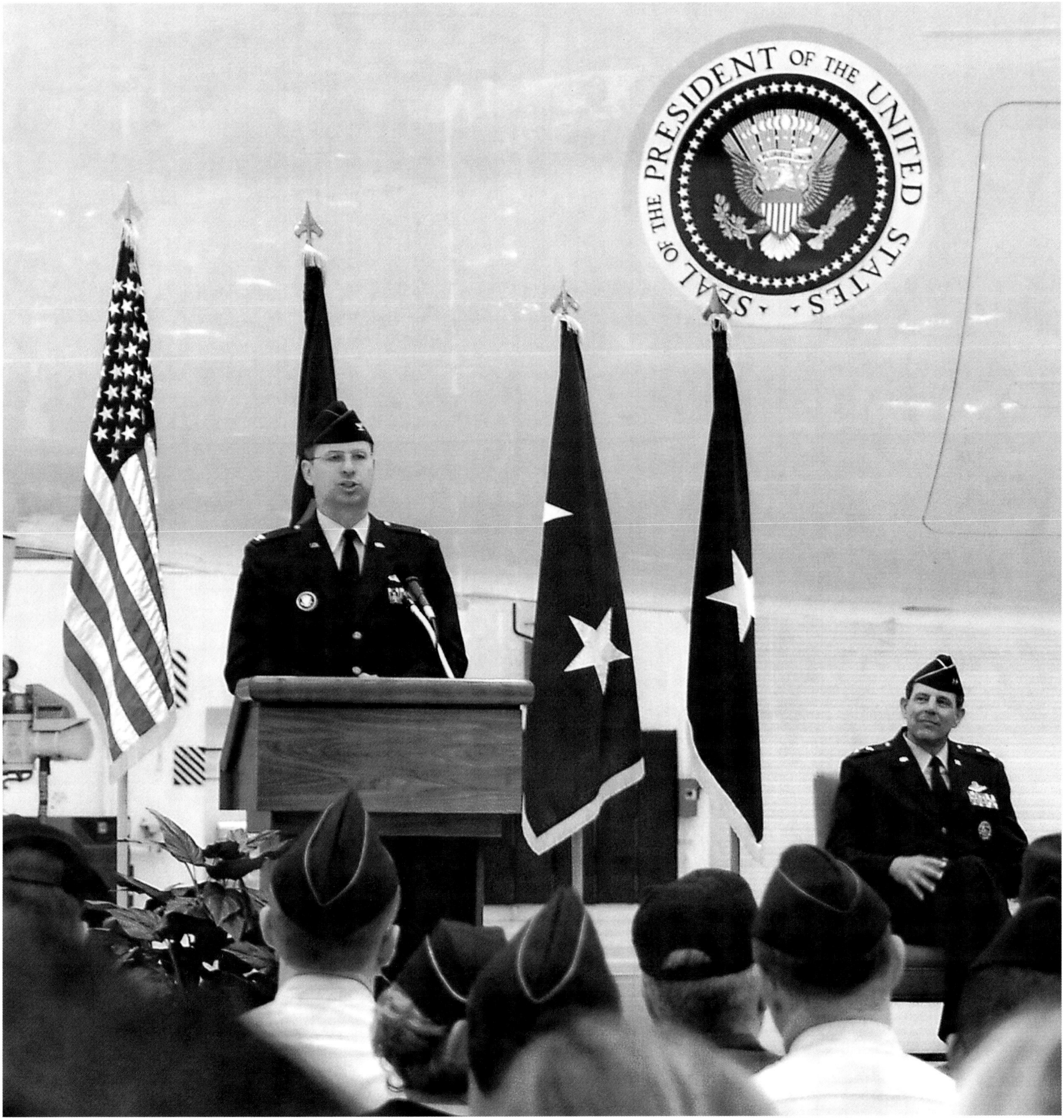
SEAL OF THE PRESIDENT OF THE UNITED STATES

In 2001, the Air Force retired SAM 27000, the long-serving C-137C (Boeing 707-353B) that had been the presidential aircraft for Presidents Nixon, Ford, Carter, Reagan, and (briefly) the elder George Bush. After being known to the public as Air Force One from 1972 until 1990, the VC-137C lost its "V" prefix and its presidential role, but it continued to transport dignitaries with the 89th Airlift Wing. The C-137C is slated to become part of the Ronald Reagan Presidential Library in Simi Valley, California. *John Gourley*

been a part of hundreds more presidential missions. His involvement with the presidential unit has spanned three administrations, and his flights have crossed numerous countries, including China, Pakistan, and Turkey.

The former deputy commander of the Presidential Airlift Group, Colonel Mark Tillman, replaces Donnelly to become the 12th presidential pilot and the new PAG commander, just six months into the George W. Bush administration. Tillman has already notched up a long list of achievements, including efforts to redesign the interior of the presidential VC-25As. When delivered, the presidential aircraft already have been

hardened against electrons that might bombard them as a result of a nuclear detonation—the so-called EMP, or electromagnetic pulse. With a new century unfolding, Air Force One's typewriters have given way to computers, its telephone consoles to hand-held phones, and its communications equipment to newer, more secure software. Under the Tillman regime, the VC-25As will enjoy some protection not only from atomic warfare but also from information warfare.

MORE CHANGES

As for the wing commander, Hawkins is given a second star and moves up in the Air Force to become

vice director of the Pentagon's joint staff. Hawkins is replaced on August 15, 2001, by Colonel Glenn F. Spears (likely to become a brigadier general quickly), an experienced airlift veteran and VIP pilot. On his first tour as commander of the 140,000 square foot compound where Air Force One resides—in high-ceilinged hangars behind surveillance cameras, motion detectors, and other security gadgetry—Spears speaks with airmen who work on and maintain the VC-25A and pronounces himself "pleased and honored" to have the 89th Airlift Wing's top job.

Spears came to Andrews from the Pentagon, where he served as executive officer to Air Force Chief of Staff General Michael E. Ryan (who retired after four years in the service's top job a few days later). Speaking of Air Force One and of the wing that flies the president, Spears said, "The 89th is a very well-running wing. I have no intention of coming in to stir things up." Spears is a command pilot with over 3,100 flight hours in B-1B Lancer and B-52D/G/H Stratofortress bombers, KC-135A/Q/R/T Stratotankers, and the MC-130H Combat Talon special operations version of the Hercules transport.

Like the new presidential pilot, the new wing commander will have plenty of heavy responsibility. Air Force One is only one of his concerns, of course,

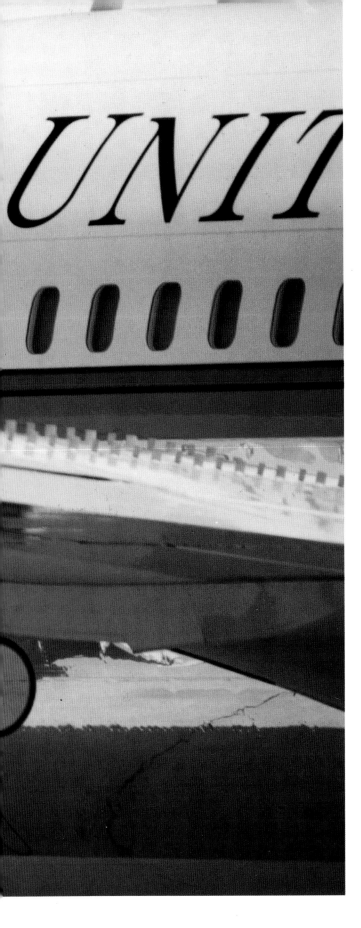

but it enjoys priority. While the blue and white Boeing 747s have remained unchanged since they were delivered to Spears' wing eleven years earlier, they are undergoing constant changes on the inside.

THE OLD AND THE NEW

On August 30, 2001, President George W. Bush makes the final presidential flight in SAM 27000, the VC-137C or Boeing 707-353B that served seven presidents, including his father. Making a one-day jaunt to San Antonio, Texas, Bush uses the aircraft that took Richard Nixon home to California and ferried Jimmy Carter to Germany to greet American hostages from Iran. This is the very last time this aging but much-loved aircraft will use the radio call sign Air Force One. Briefly, during Nixon's tenure, the aircraft was also known as the *The Spirit of '76*.

"It will carry no more presidents, but it will carry forever the spirit of American democracy," Bush says of the aircraft. He is making his only flight on the aircraft as president.

This is also the aircraft that became stuck in the mud when taxiing with Bill Clinton aboard during a routine trip to Willard Airport near Champaign, Illinois, in May 1998, but no one is recalling that day. A retirement ceremony for the aircraft in San Antonio is canceled due to heavy rains there. The event is moved to a hangar at Texas State Technical College, near Waco, instead.

SAM 27000 has flown 444 missions as Air Force One, covering a million miles. It was used constantly by Ronald Reagan and will now be on indefinite loan to the Reagan library in Simi Valley, California, as part of an exhibit on presidential aircraft.

At the Texas ceremony to commemorate the end of the career of this aircraft are former presidential pilots Ralph Albertazzie, Bob Ruddick, and Danny Barr, as well as Chief Master Sergeant Joe Chappell, the flight engineer who was aboard the aircraft on its virgin trip from the Boeing factory to Andrews back in 1972.

The defensive system against heat-seeking missiles on SAM 27000 was known in jargon as the infrared countermeasures self-defense system (ISDS) and was developed from an earlier system called the AN/ALQ-144. The ISDS was a fuselage-or pylon-mounted item designed to provide protection from anti-aircraft missiles employing infrared homing devices. On the presidential VC-137Cs, the system was contained in rearward-facing fairings immediately above the rear of each of the planes' four engines, seen here culminating in violet, mirror-like disks. *John Gourley*

Opposite page: This portrait of SAM 28000 inside its compound gives some idea of the fences that surround Air Force One's hangars and the area around the aircraft. Not visible but also present are surveillance cameras, motion detectors, and other security devices. *Charles Taylor*

There are no bigger fans of presidential aircraft—or of the hard-working 89th Airlift Wing—than the author and publishers of this volume. But the story has warts as well as beauty marks. They are sprinkled among the preceding pages.

The 89th is accustomed to being accused of being too ostentatious. Even a former presidential pilot told the author, "I don't really understand why the president needs such a big, fancy plane." There is little cause for worry. Congress, press, and public accept Air Force One as it is. There may be a danger in the opposite direction. When it purchased the Boeing 757 (C-32A), which George W. Bush has used as Air Force One, the Air Force nixed a plan to acquire at a reasonable price the far more capable Boeing 767.

Back in the 1980s, the 89th Wing took flak from press and public (and the minority side in Congress) when it planned to earmark an aircraft, a C-20H Gulfstream IV, for the Speaker of the House of Representatives.

Few Americans believe that Air Force One makes the president too aloof or haughty, but some wonder about the culture that is evolving around the great aircraft.

WHITE HOUSE STUFF

For one thing, there is the isolation of the Presidential Airlift Group from the rest of the 89th Wing, from the rest of Andrews, and from the rest of the Air Force. The 89th is the only wing that requires two flying groups, one for the president and one for everybody else. Some observers say that those who maintain, crew, and pilot Air Force One spend too long in their tours of duty, separating them from the rest of the military—to whom they do, in fact, seem aloof.

On another level, it sometimes seems that those who maintain and fly Air Force One get caught up in the sort of jargon they might never use if they were not hanging around with the Secret Service. In recent years, Air Force security forces coordinating with the Secret Service have begun using code

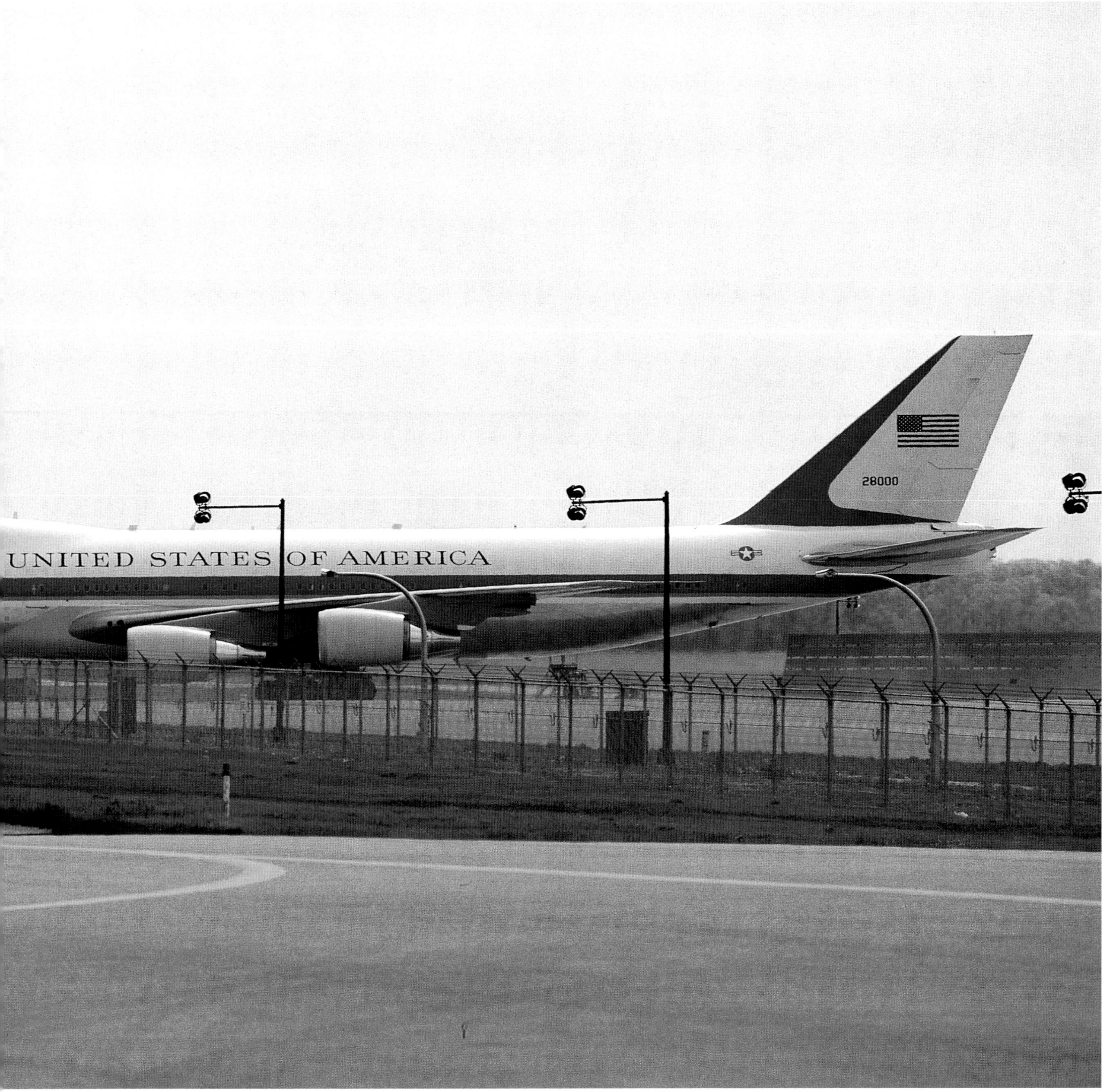
28000
UNITED STATES OF AMERICA

words that sound like they come from a low-budget spy movie. Samples:

ARMORED PRESIDENTIAL LIMO
Stagecoach

CAMP DAVID
Buckeye

DULLES AIRPORT
Coach House

MOTORCADE FOLLOW VEHICLE
Halfback

MOTOR POOL
Carpet

NATIONAL AIRPORT
Curbside

SECRETARY OF THE TREASURY
Fencing Master

STATE DEPARTMENT
Fireside

STATE DEPARTMENT SECURITY OFFICE
Foghorn

STATE DEPARTMENT SECURITY VEHICLE
Fullback

SURVEILLANCE HELICOPTER
Huntsman

WHITE HOUSE SITUATION ROOM
Cement Mixer

Jargon is, of course, everywhere in the world of Air Force One. The Marine Corps VH-3D carrying the chief executive may be Marine One when the president is aboard, but the rest of the time it uses the call sign Nighthawk (the nickname of squadron HMX-1) with a number. Andrews Air Force Base becomes Acrobat on the radio. Phoenix Copper is the call sign for an aircraft carrying the first lady. Phoenix Banner is the call sign for an aircraft carrying presidential equipment.

Air Force and other military people have picked up the Secret Service jargon used to identify individuals. President George W. Bush is called "Ranger" in radio conversation. Bill Clinton was "Eagle," Hillary

The famous presidential helicopter Marine One, better known as Sikorsky VH-60N (bureau number 163260) of helicopter squadron VMX-1, the "Nighthawks." *John Gourley*

Clinton was "Evergreen," and daughter Chelsea was "Energy." The elder George Bush was "Timberwolf," Ronald Reagan was "Rawhide," and Jimmy Carter was "Deacon." One-time presidential candidate Bob Dole became "Patriot" in radio jargon.

Those who work on, maintain, and fly Air Force One seem not to have noticed that they are succumbing to the passion for insider terminology that happens in any clique. Are they becoming too isolated from the outside world, too far out of touch with the America they serve? Not many think so yet, but the growing size and exclusivity of the Presidential Airlift Group has come to the attention of some.

Polls show that Americans distrust Congress but trust the military. Americans get angry when congressmen receive perks, but not when the president travels in style. Anecdotal evidence and interviews support what the polls say. The average American is happy with the way the chief executive is transported. To underscore a point the 89th Wing makes repeatedly, Americans view Air Force One as more than a vehicle for their chief of state. As suggested above, Americans view the aircraft as an ambassador of goodwill for the nation.

MARINE ONE

Also backing up the confidence of the American people (and perhaps a little less enamored of in-house Secret Service jargon), the Executive Flight Detachment of Marine squadron HMX-1 "Nighthawks," located at the former Naval Air Station Anacostia along the Potomac River, continues to provide the president with helicopter transport. At the start of a new century, HMX-1 is equipped with two types of aircraft, the Sikorsky VH-3D Sea King and the VH-60N Blackhawk. Because of their distinctive color schemes, these helicopters are sometimes referred to as "White Tops." The 89th Wing's UH-1N Huey helicopters are available to assist in an emergency—including a wartime evacuation—but only the Marines routinely lift the president.

The VH-3D is capable of transporting 14 people and is the primary helicopter used for presidential travel, as well as for the vice president and visiting heads of state. The VH-60N seats up to 11 passengers and is used for various White House missions. Both helicopters require a pilot, copilot, and crew chief, and the VH-60N also carries a communications systems operator. The VH-60N is smaller than the VH-3D, and, because it folds easily for loading onto an Air Force C-5A/B Galaxy transport, it is ideal for overseas assignments on short notice. The HMX-1 Marines can prepare a VH-60N for loading on a C-5 in less than two hours.

The VH-3D has been in use for almost a quarter century, the VH-60N for more than a decade. An extensive Special Progressive Aircraft Rework at predetermined intervals, plus a review of the communications and navigation systems every three or four years, keep these aircraft in peak condition. No plan is on the horizon for a replacement, although the Marines are thinking more than a little about a possible presidential version of the V-22 Osprey tilt-rotor aircraft.

SAM 27000

On Saturday, September 8, 2001, SAM 27000, a former Air Force One plane, flies its final mission. Passengers aboard SAM 27000 on the flight from Andrews Air Force Base, Maryland, to San Bernardino, California, are Air Force Secretary James Roche and 30 other dignitaries. Also on the flight are 11 former members of the Air Force One flight crew. The half-dozen media folk include Hugh Sidey of *Time* magazine, Campbell Brown of NBC News, and this author. Add a crew of 15, and 63 souls are inside the plane's 153-foot fuselage, making a journey into history.

Now replaced by larger aircraft, this famous plane carried every American president since 1972. It logged 2,798 flight hours carrying chief executives 1,314,596 miles. It took Richard Nixon on his triumphant opening to China and carried him home in disgrace when he resigned. Aboard this aircraft, Jimmy Carter flew to Europe in 1981 to greet American hostages being released from Iran. Aboard this aircraft, former flight attendant Howie Franklin once struggled in vain to awaken Bill Clinton at 3:30 A.M. Washington time, finally grabbing the president forcibly by the shoulders and shouting: "You've got to get your ass out of bed!" The 42nd president rose, grinned, and responded, "Oh. Okay."

Today, the plane is carrying memories of seven presidents and of a long, blue line of pilots, navigators, flight engineers, communicators, flight attendants, and maintainers—the Air Force people behind Air Force One.

A crowd of a few dozen watches our departure from Andrews. Two thousand people, a band, and a gaggle of local bigwigs greet us on arrival at San Bernardino. But despite the many people on the scene in person and in spirit, this day belongs to just one man.

This is Ronald Reagan's day.

Aboard this aircraft, Reagan flew to Berlin and exhorted, "Mr. Gorbachev, tear down this wall."

"When he walked in, you knew you were seeing the president," remembers former flight engineer William "Joe" Chappell. "He had a presence."

"What a nice man," says former flight attendant John Haigh. "The stresses of the job aged some presidents. Not Reagan. The job energized him. And whether you were a prime minister or the elevator operator in a hotel where he was staying, he never failed to have something nice to say."

Of 445 presidential missions flown by SAM 27000, Reagan was the passenger on 211. The breakdown for other presidents is: Nixon, 30; Ford, 55; Carter, 86; Bush, 57; Clinton, 5, and the second Bush, one. Sheer numbers make this Reagan's airplane, but once it's placed on display, the former Air Force One will be accessible to all Americans.

It is Reagan's day, but the 40th president is not here—sidetracked, finally, by the ravages of Alzheimer's disease. His presence commands the scene, nonetheless.

When we taxi in, former First Lady Nancy Reagan comes aboard SAM 27000 and greets everyone on the plane. She looks smaller in person, not physically strong, yet holding up nobly under many burdens. She recognizes former crew members. Several rate a hug.

There are speeches by Secretary Roche, Nancy Reagan, and others. SAM 27000 will now be dismantled in San Bernardino and trucked to the hilltop Reagan Presidential Library, 50 miles northwest of Los Angeles. Eventually, the plane will be reassembled inside a structure that will blend with the library's Spanish architecture.

Franklin, Chappell, and Haigh say they enjoyed cordiality with every president. Of course, politics plays some role in Air Force presidential operations. But, for these former crew members, politics stayed on the ground when Air Force One lifted off. Franklin tells his Clinton anecdote with affection. Haigh speaks of the often-aloof Richard Nixon with warmth.

Yes, this happy occasion is Ronald Reagan's day. But it is also a day for the Air Force community. On SAM 27000's final flight, the top Air Force figure is Roche. At the other end of the spectrum are three staff sergeants on today's flight crew—flying crew chiefs Richard Balfour and Allan Blancaflor, and flight attendant Pamela Varon. Among others on this final flight are the pilots, Lieutenant Colonels James T. Robinson and Daniel K. Brunskole; navigator, Lieutenant Colonel George Pavelko; and flight engineer, Technical Sergeant John Mancuso.

Everyone contributes. Everyone celebrates. The occasion is a joyous one. There is a mood of festivity when SAM 27000 is left in California and the party flies home aboard C-32A 92-0004. At this happy time, no one has a clue what will happen to Air Force One and to the nation about sixty hours later.

PEARL HARBOR II

On September 11, 2001, the date of the most destructive attack ever carried out against the United States, Air Force One takes the president of the

United States on an unprecedented three travel legs for the first time in history. The VC-25A aircraft is SAM 28000. On this day, the other ship, SAM 29000, is temporarily at the Boeing facility in Wichita, Kansas, for maintenance.

For the first time, fighters escort Air Force One while it is carrying President George W. Bush. The F-16C Fighting Falcons of the 121st Fighter Squadron, District of Columbia Air National Guard, are there because the White House has learned that terrorists may attempt to ram the VC-25A with a hijacked airliner.

To Americans, the date will be etched in memory forever—the unforgettable television images of airliners slamming into buildings, the Hollywood-style pyrotechnics, the death and horror and tragedy. To some, the American style of abbreviating dates is appropriate: The day is also nine, one, one.

Here are the basics, never to be forgotten by most of us:

8:45 A.M. EST: American Airlines Flight 11, a Boeing 767, which departed at 7:59 A.M. on a flight from Boston to Los Angeles carrying 92 people, including 5 hijackers, 2 pilots, and 9 flight attendants, flies into the north tower of New York's World Trade Center.

9:03 A.M. EST: United Airlines Flight 175, a Boeing 767-200, which departed at 7:58 A.M. on a flight from Boston to Los Angeles carrying 65 people, including 5 hijackers, 2 pilots, and 7 flight attendants, hits the south tower of the World Trade Center.

9:45 A.M. EST: American Flight 77, a Boeing 757, which departed at 8:10 A.M. from Washington, D.C.'s, Dulles International Airport for Los Angeles carrying 64 people including 4 hijackers, 2 pilots, and 4 flight attendants, dives toward the White House. The plane is boring down toward the Executive Mansion from the south of the Pentagon Building when it pulls a 270-degree turn before slamming into the west wall of the Pentagon.

9:55 A.M. EST: The south tower of the World Trade Center collapses.

10:00 A.M. EST: United Flight 93, a Boeing 757-200, which departed at 8:01 A.M. from Newark to San Francisco carrying 45 people including 4 hijackers, 2 pilots, and 5 flight attendants, crashes in Stony Creek Township, Pennsylvania, apparently after passengers attempt to overpower hijackers. Later, White House officials will tell reporters that the hijackers of this aircraft may have intended to ram a landmark in Washington or ram Air Force One, President Bush's VC-25A.

When the attack begins, Bush is in Sarasota, Florida, about to speak to young students about education. Air Force One is at nearby MacDill Air Force Base, near Tampa. Bush cuts short his Florida visit. Air Force One takes off, the intention being to return Bush to Washington.

As the attack on the United States unfolds, for the first time in history the government activates the "Senex" program, also called the CoG (Continuity of Government) program or the PSSS (Presidential Successor Support System). The program is super-secret. Apart from the brief allusion to events surrounding the attempted assassination of President Reagan appearing in the first chapter, almost nothing is known about how it works. When asked about the program on September 8, only three days earlier, 89th Airlift Wing commander Colonel Glenn Spears shakes his head and says, "I can't answer that." Suffice to say that shortly after 8:45 A.M., while cable news cameras are focused on the World Trade Center, steps are made to guard the succession to the White House.

As Air Force One takes off in Florida, officials conclude that the hijacked American Flight 77 is being aimed like a cruise missile at the White House. Secret Service agents circulate among the staff in the Executive Mansion urging employees to leave the building calmly and quietly. Then, their demeanor changes. The agents move more quickly. One of them cries, "Never mind about being calm. Just run. Get out, now." Dozens pour out of the president's home and offices. Flight 77, which has

Air Force One overhead. *Charles Taylor*

been in the air for an hour since taking off a few miles away, is now boring toward the nation's capital.

Aware of this, officials decide to divert Air Force One. Moreover, officials conclude that Air Force One is itself threatened. The VC-25A climbs to 41,000 feet, higher than it usually flies, perhaps complicating the geometric problem for anyone plotting to converge with the presidential aircraft. Now, the fighter escort appears. The decision is made to divert Air Force One to Barksdale Air Force Base, Louisiana.

The two men next in line for the presidency, Vice President Dick Cheney and Speaker of the House Dennis Hastert, are rushed to secret locations via undisclosed means—Hastert, possibly by land, or possibly by C-20C Gulfstream IIIs or UH-1N Hueys belonging to the 89th. Later, the nation is told Cheney was in a location deep beneath the White House.

Flight 77 alters course and dives at the Pentagon. Contrary to virtually all published reports, it does not fly into the building. It flies into the ground at the helipad, a few feet from the building, and bounces into the structure.

Bush is diverted again, and Air Force One hauls him from Barksdale to U.S. Strategic Command headquarters at Offutt Air Force Base, Nebraska.

At some point, apparently during the stay at Offutt, a decision is reached that the threat has passed. Air Force One takes off again. With Manhattan and the Pentagon in flames, Bush understands that he will transmit an important message by returning to Washington and demonstrating that the government is intact. Cheney and Hastert also return to Washington. The VC-25A lands at Andrews.

Bush's return to the White House aboard the Sikorsky VH-3D, Marine One, is orchestrated somewhat differently than a typical arrival. Looking to the sky for Bush's helicopter, observers see not a single helicopter but eight, approaching in formation. If there is a threat to Marine One, how will the foe know which helicopter to attack? In the

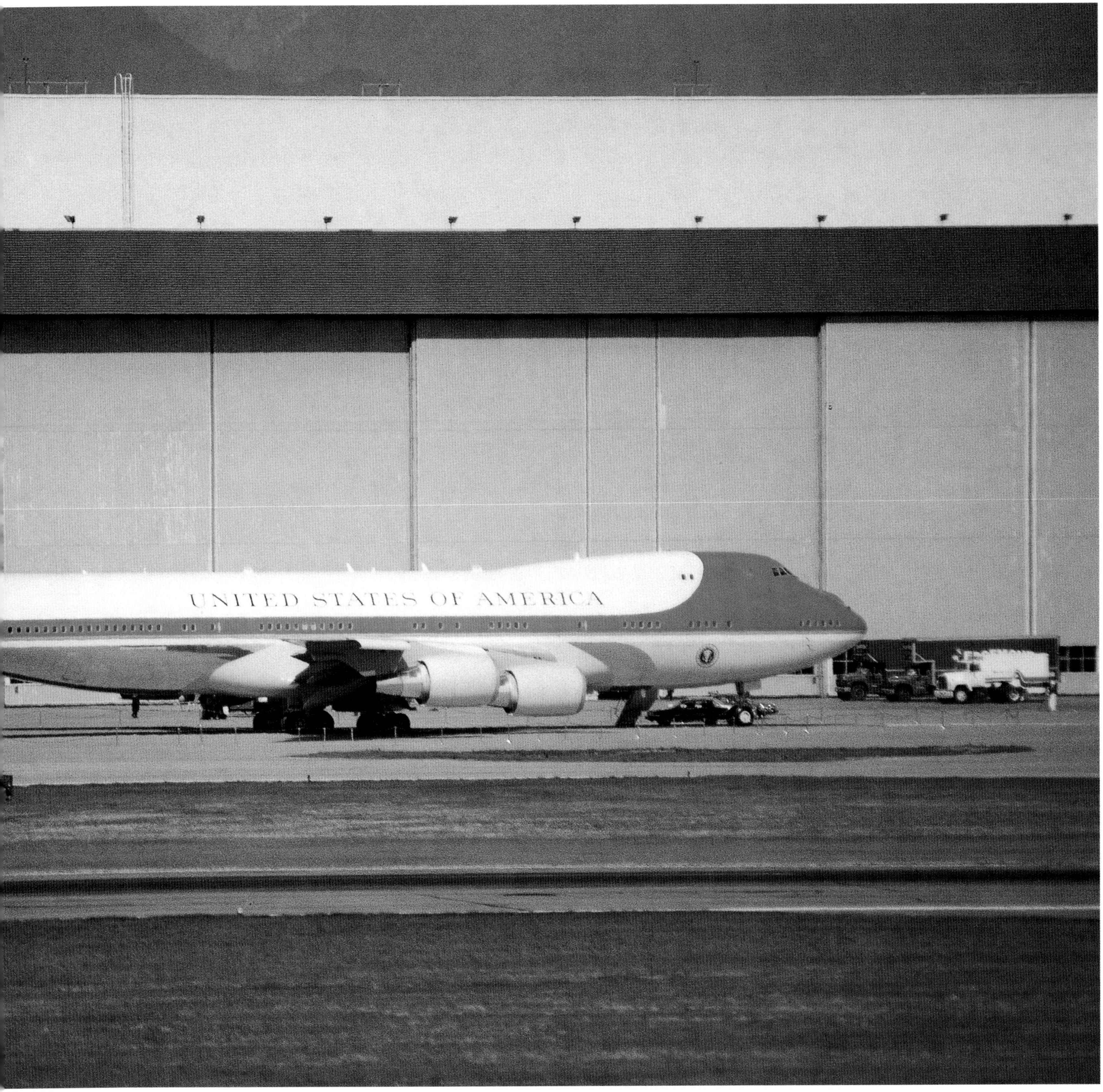
UNITED STATES OF AMERICA

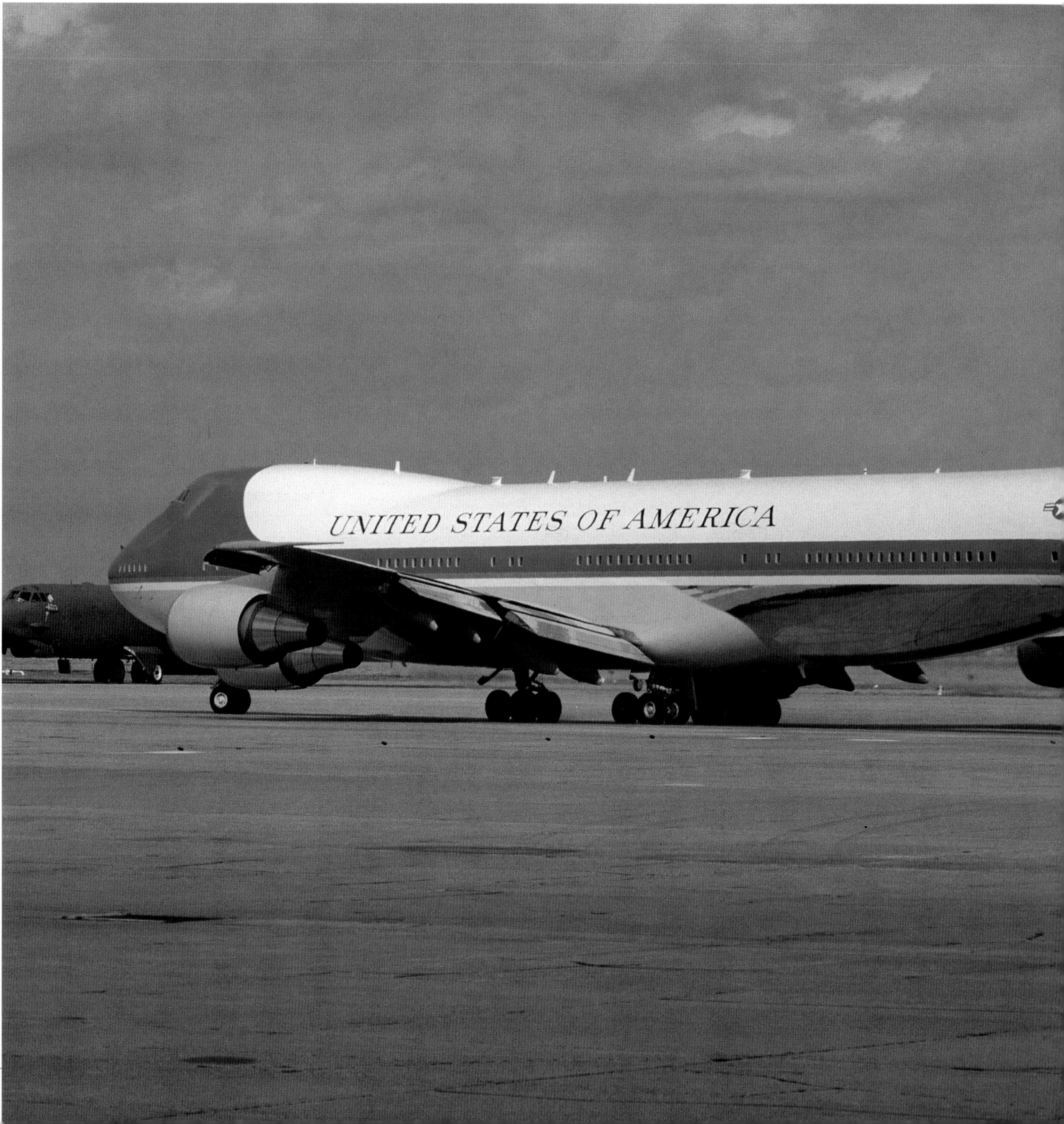
UNITED STATES OF AMERICA

end, no threat materializes, the VH-3D touches down, and Bush strides to the Oval Office—to address the nation later in the day.

A NEW ERA

The terrorist attack on September 11, 2001, was a turning point in the nation's history. Americans will remember their lives before September 11, 2001. They will remember their lives after. It is fashionable to say of such a date that it was the day we lost our innocence. That would be the wrong interpretation for adversaries to make of the American psyche. The nation's foes have never understood that freedom and innocence are not the same thing. In an interview on September 15, four days after the attack, amid the most pervasive security measures ever instituted at Andrews, 89th Wing commander Colonel Glenn Spears tells the author, "This will be a new time for us." That day, a C-20B Gulfstream III is using the radio call sign Air Force One, carrying Bush on a visit that will take him to Manhattan to view the worst destruction ever inflicted on America in a single day.

Before that turning point, Air Force One was becoming a little more accessible to press and public, and outsiders were being permitted to see a little more of the details of the plane's interior. Afterward, new security measures took hold. Yes, Air Force One would continue to serve as an ambassador of a great nation. But now the role of the aircraft in assuring the president's safety would take priority.

The task of transporting the president by air has always been a military task—a military challenge. In today's new era, it will continue to be so. The Boeing 747, alias VC-25A, alias Air Force One, is, in the end, not merely an ambassador but also a part of the nation's arsenal. In easy times and in difficult times, Air Force One serves America well.

Aircraft 92-9000, alias SAM 29000, taxies past another aircraft built by the same manufacturer, a B-52H Stratofortress. The backup Air Force One is carrying President Bill Clinton to Barksdale Air Force Base, Louisiana on February 8, 1994. Both the rear of the engine pylons and the rear of the fuselage itself apparently hold defensive countermeasures, none of which the Air Force will discuss. *Greg L. Davis*

INDEX